Lessons Learned from
a Life on Trial

Lessons Learned from a Life on Trial

Landmark Cases from a Veteran Litigator and What They Can Teach Trial Lawyers

DANIEL SMALL

AMERICAN**BAR**ASSOCIATION

ABA Publishing

Printed in the United States of America.

28 27 26 25 24   5 4 3 2 1

Library of Congress Cataloging-in-Publication Data

Names: Small, Daniel I., 1954- author.
Title: Lessons learned from a life on trial : landmark cases from a veteran
    litigator and what they can teach trial lawyers / author, Daniel Small.
Description: 1st edition. | Chicago : American Bar Association, ABA
    Publishing, Section Flagship, 2024. | Summary: "I learned a great deal
    about trials from the lawyers that I worked with in the US Attorney's
    Office that summer, and from many mentors and experiences since. But
    perhaps the most important thing I learned, is that if one really wants
    to be a trial lawyer, it's just not something that can be learned from a
    book, or in a classroom. Certainly, those things can help, and I have
    been fortunate to teach trial practice courses at Harvard and elsewhere
    around the world. But true trial practice comes mostly from watching,
    listening, asking questions, practicing, and doing it-with all of the
    triumphs and tragedies that go along with trial work. Nowhere is the
    phrase "practicing law" more accurate than in trial work, where we spend
    a lifetime learning and practicing, on a journey without an endpoint"–
    Provided by publisher.
Identifiers: LCCN 2023045885 | ISBN 9781639054190 (paperback) |
    ISBN 9781639054206 (ebook)
Subjects: LCSH: Trial practice--United States. | Trial practice--United
    States--Cases. | Lawyers--United States.
Classification: LCC KF8915.S57 2024 | DDC 347.73/7--dc23/eng/20231003
LC record available at https://lccn.loc.gov/2023045885

Discounts are available for books ordered in bulk. Special consideration is given to state bars, CLE programs, and other bar-related organizations. Inquire at Book Publishing, ABA Publishing, American Bar Association, 321 N. Clark Street, Chicago, Illinois 60654-7598.

www.shopABA.org

Contents

Introduction

We each find our own path in our own way. Some trial lawyers know what they want to be from a very tender age, perhaps influenced by family or friends, perhaps by movies, TV, or other sources. I had no such history. I was supposed to be a teacher. Several great teaching experiences culminated in a part-time job teaching during my senior year in college at a program in Boston called Metropathways, which brought high school kids from the inner city and the suburbs together one day a week. I taught an interactive course in politics and government. I loved it—loved the challenges and loved the kids.

The program offered me a full-time teaching job when I graduated from college, and I accepted. They told me that having a Harvard degree was nice, but if I actually wanted to be paid slightly more than the ridiculous pittance they were offering, I should get my teacher certification (which Harvard did not provide). So, I went out west for the summer after graduation and took graduate courses in secondary education at the University of Colorado at Boulder. Then three things happened.

First, when I returned to Boston from Colorado, eager to start teaching, I learned that the program—at the last minute—had not received its matching funding, so there was no program that year and there was no job for me. I was fortunate to find exciting roles at Harvard's Institute of Politics and Kennedy School of Government during the next year. Gradually, although I continued to love teaching (and still do), the plan to do it full-time somewhat faded. Unsure of what else to do, or what kind of law I might want to practice, I nevertheless went to law school.

Second, after my first year of law school, I wangled through some political connections and gained a summer internship at the United States Attorney's Office in Boston. It had never occurred to me to be a prosecutor. Indeed, my family's and my own political leanings made it a very strange, and strained, choice. But I was curious. I had taken a trial practice course in law school, but truly had no clear idea what it meant to be a trial lawyer in real cases. Fortunately, I was assigned to work principally with a young, up-and-coming assistant US attorney who happened to have several great trials that summer. Standing in the well of the courtroom after a long and exhausting trial day, I looked around and said to myself: "This is it. This is what I want to do."

Third, as the saying goes, "Sometimes the best results come when you are thrown in the deep end." I was fortunate to have that experience. Coming out of law school, I turned down a job with a great private firm to accept a Trial Attorney position with the Criminal Division of the US Department of Justice (DOJ). Although based in Washington, DC, my principal job was to travel the country investigating, developing, and trying cases for the department. As a result of twists and turns that could only happen in the government, I did very quickly get thrown into the deep end on several challenging and significant cases and, to a great extent, had to learn by doing. Many of those experiences form the basis for some of these stories.

I learned a great deal about trials from the lawyers whom I worked with in the US Attorney's Office that summer in Boston and from many mentors and experiences since then, but perhaps the most important thing I learned is that if someone wants to be a trial lawyer, it's not something that can be learned from a book or in a classroom. Certainly those things can help, and I have been fortunate to teach trial practice courses at Harvard and elsewhere around the world, but true trial practice comes mostly from watching, listening, asking questions, practicing, and doing it—with all of the triumphs and tragedies that go along with trial work. Nowhere is the phrase "practicing law" more accurate than in trial work, where we spend a lifetime learning and practicing while on a journey without an endpoint.

Trials are hard work. The popular image of a lawyer standing up and "winging it" in court is, in reality, often an invitation for disaster. Certainly there are moments in any trial that require spontaneity, but spontaneity generally only succeeds with careful preparation. The famous trial lawyer Vincent Bugliosi put it well: "It's simply not possible to powerfully articulate a great number of points, one immediately following another, extemporaneously. There is a best way to make a point, and to find it takes time and sweat on the yellow pad."[1]

When I do teach trial practice or other aspects of litigation now, including my witness preparation work, I often find myself trying to help people understand a point I'm making by relaying a story from real-life trials. Recently, I came home from doing such a program in Dallas and was telling one of the stories to my wife, Alix. She has patiently heard many of my stories over and over again, but this happened to be one that she had not heard. When I finished, she commented that many of the stories that I use when I speak or teach are both interesting and contain useful lessons for other trial lawyers. She suggested that I start writing down these stories to preserve them and find a way to share them with others.

I was skeptical. By happenstance, my law firm had recently distributed very nice hardcover spiral-bound journal books with the Holland & Knight name inscribed on the cover. I'm not sure why they did this: there are probably only a very few of us who actually write things out by hand anymore. However, I am most grateful to whoever made that decision. I was able to ask around and accumulate several of these journal books from colleagues who weren't going to use them. At the same time, I had several cross-country airplane flights for cases on the West Coast. To my surprise and delight, I found that—at least for me—writing is a great way to pass the time in flight. So, I followed my wife's advice, and I started writing about some of my cases.

On one flight, I pulled out the journal book and pen before the plane left the ground, wrote for the entire flight, and finally put the tools of the trade away as the plane was landing. I had not spoken to the very nice lady in the next seat the whole flight, but as we were landing and I was putting things away, she turned to me and said, "You must love to write, you've been writing the whole flight!" She's quite right, and the process of remembering, revisiting, and writing down some of these extraordinary experiences has in itself been worthwhile and rewarding to me.

However, there are several challenges that I discovered in doing this.

---

[1] Vincent Bugliosi and Bruce Henderson, *And the Sea Will Tell* (W.W. Norton and Company 1991).

The first is memory: I have been fortunate enough to be trying cases for many years, so some of these cases are quite old. I made little or no effort to dig out transcripts, pleadings, and other documents to corroborate my recitation of the case. This is not an attempt at an accurate history but rather an effort to relay experiences that may help teach useful lessons. Any mistakes—and undoubtedly there are some—or even artistic license to make the stories clearer are strictly the fault of the author, and I apologize to all others involved.

The second is privilege. I have had the honor of representing some extraordinary people as their counsel, but with that honor comes the tight restraints of the attorney-client privilege. The how and why of many things that happened during cases, particularly in private practice, must necessarily remain cloaked in the privilege. As a result, some key cases and important stories received short shrift or no mention at all.

The third is people. As trial lawyers, we learn from each other, and I've been lucky to learn from some great trial lawyers and judges. Much of what I know about this strange process I learned from watching and listening to others. I owe debts of gratitude I can never fully repay to them. I also owe gratitude to my wife, Alix, and my children Bailey, Schuyler, and Gabrielle for providing me with love, support, and encouragement, and putting up with my many absences and distractions. Just like being a trial lawyer, I had to put in the work to be an author. This book is one way for me to say thanks to all who helped make it happen.

Prologue

The word *trial:* "Act or process of testing," from Anglo-Fr. trial, noun formed from triet "to try." *Try:* from Gallo-Rom. triare, of unknown origin, Ground sense: "separate out (the good) by examination."[1] This book attempts to entertain, explore, and share lessons from this process of examination. Throughout many of these stories and lessons learned run three general core themes:

1. Know your court.
2. Tell your story.
3. Do the right thing.

I was fortunate to learn these core themes at the very beginning of my career in, of all places, the US Magistrate's Court in Hyattsville, Maryland. Generally, federal magistrates work in US courthouses and take care of a wide range of hearings, motions, discovery, and other matters. But in the Washington, DC, area, there are so many federal roads, parks, buildings—you name it—that they created a separate Magistrate's Court for Hyattsville. That small courthouse has a full-time magistrate, court reporter, clerk's office, and other essential parts of a working courthouse. It is basically a permanent traffic and misdemeanor court. However, there is no full-time prosecutor. At some point, the magistrate agreed with the US Department of Justice (DOJ) to have a program where new lawyers at the Department would come and act as the prosecutor in his court for a period of time as training. My vague recollection is that it was six weeks.

It was quite an intimidating experience at first. You would get in at about seven or eight in the morning, and there would be a stack of fifty

---

[1] Quelle: www.etymonline.com; s.a. Weigend, *Harvard Journal of Law & Public Policy,* 2003, Vol. 26.

or more case files on your desk. You would spend the next hour or two walking through the files with the various law enforcement officers who were involved in the cases. They would be from an alphabet soup range of federal enforcement agencies. The point was to get a feel for what cases were important, which officers you could best rely on, and what the real issues were.

While I studied the files and met with the officers, a crowd would start to build in the courtroom and the outside corridor with defendants, families, friends, lawyers, and others waiting for court to get underway. At some point, I would walk out into the courtroom and introduce myself: "I am Assistant United States Attorney Daniel Small. I will be handling all the cases for the government today. If any of you would like to 'discuss your case' before court begins, please form a line starting at the bar." And a long line would form spreading out of the courtroom and into the hallway. One by one, you would meet with the defendants and their lawyer, if they had one. Some people wanted to object until you suggested that objecting was of course their right, but it meant that their case would proceed to trial later that day. Some people wanted to give excuses or at least beg for mercy on the amount of the fine or the points on their insurance. In the right circumstances—and there was of course an endless variety—there were certain adjustments that I had the freedom to give. Sometimes I would go back into chambers and ask the magistrate for guidance or permission. If we couldn't resolve the matter, I could simply say that we will put this up for consideration when the judge takes the bench.

Soon enough, the magistrate, who had been back in his chambers having coffee and going through his paperwork, would get impatient and come out on the bench. It was an extraordinary experience for a brand-new lawyer: We would try at least several cases a day, although many trials were little more than, "And what happened next, officer?" But I was on my feet, looking through case files, reading the law and the witness statements, questioning witnesses, trying cases, and resolving matters. In some cases where defendants had questions, they would be dealt with by the magistrate, and then if the magistrate, in going through his list, got to someone who clearly had not had the opportunity to "discuss their case" with me, the magistrate would suggest that he put their case off until after the next break so they would have an opportunity to do so.

Everyone who worked in the courthouse knew that I was just a beginner, and many of them were extraordinarily helpful to me, particularly the magistrate, from whom I learned a great deal. That included the three core themes.

1. KNOW YOUR COURT

Like many courthouses around the country, there was a group of lawyers who focused on the Hyattsville Magistrate's Court and spent much of their time there. Relationships were generally very cordial all around: after all, this was not really life or death, and everyone knew that you would be working together on other cases tomorrow, so you had to be able to trust each other today. Besides, there was that local barroom where courthouse folks liked to hang out together and share stories and amber liquids at the end of the week. Naturally, over time, these courthouse lawyers got to know not only the people but also the local rules—written and unwritten. Every court has its own unwritten rules. Justice can hardly survive or be efficient without them. In this courthouse, that included the fact that many of the crimes we were dealing with had prison terms written into the statute of up to a year (anything more would not be a misdemeanor). These were technical maximums, not real-life sentences. It was, to say least, rare that anyone went to jail for just running a stop sign, but many people don't know that.

Over time, there had evolved a set of unwritten standard results for many of the common offenses. A first-time traffic offense, with no accident or injury, and a remorseful defendant who had acted reasonably with the officer could often be worked out within a certain range of fines. Of course, the lawyers who practiced in and around that courthouse knew these unwritten rules. It made working out cases much simpler: the arguments would be over mitigating or extenuating factors, background, etc., but both sides knew the general parameters.

Drunk driving, of course, was the great leveler. It cut across all socioeconomic lines and brought a wide variety of defendants into the courthouse. One time, a very high-level executive from Washington, DC, was caught drunk driving. Into our little courthouse he came with four—count them, four—lawyers from a top firm in DC. What he was paying them to defend him for this traffic offense, I can only imagine.

The problem was that for all their high fees, they knew nothing about this courthouse or its unwritten rules. When I got to him in line and it came time to "discuss their case," I found a side room where I could meet with the whole gang of them. Once settled, apparently used to being in command, the senior partner made an impassioned plea on behalf of his client (there was no real basis to dispute liability, this was all mitigation) and then he decided to take the bull by the horns and make the first offer in settlement negotiations for a plea deal.

Clearly, someone had researched the applicable statute for him and probably given him an excellent memorandum, setting forth the maximum penalties, including jail term. He had undoubtedly reassured his client that he would use his renowned influence and skills to demand a greatly reduced sentence from the maximum.

But what no one had told the senior partner, the senior partner had not bothered to find out, and the senior partner had not told the client because none of them knew the courthouse, was that I was well aware of the statute's technical maximum penalties but couldn't care less. That's just not how we based our plea agreements. For a first-time drunk driving offense, no accident, no injuries, no passengers, no damage, and immediate remorse, everyone in the courthouse knew the appropriate general range of punishment. The problem was that the range—what I as the prosecutor would recommend—was significantly *less* severe than what the high-priced counsel was recommending as his opening negotiating offer for his client. He was unwittingly selling his client down the river.

What to do? If that's what his own counsel was offering, all I had to do was to smile, say "yes," leave the room, and move on to the next case. There was, after all, still a long line waiting for me in the courtroom. I won't deny that I thought about it a bit. But I couldn't do it. Just because his lawyer didn't know the unwritten rules of the courthouse didn't mean that I didn't know them or could so easily violate them. But how do you get to a fair result without thoroughly embarrassing the senior partner? "You're an idiot, and it's putting your client at risk!" didn't seem like the diplomatic way to go. So, I hemmed and hawed for a little bit, talking about theoreticals and hypotheticals.

Ironically, it was the most junior of the four lawyers who caught on first. Perhaps because we were closer in age, although even as the most junior of the four, he was still older than I was. He started hemming and hawing with me, including about how their opening offer was really just an example of how this important statute could be abused and over-used. We never talked about unwritten rules or the importance of know-ing the practice within that court, and no one stated the obvious about how badly they had almost screwed up, but it slowly became obvious to everyone in the room. We eventually walked it back to a resolution that was within the general boundaries of that court, considerably more favorable to the defendant than what his counsel had initially "offered." Part of me felt badly for the defendant: Surely his lead counsel would go back to him and brag about what an extraordinary deal he had some-how been able to convince me to accept. When just as surely, if the poor guy had hired one of the courthouse regulars—or if his counsel had consulted with one of the regulars, not just the law books, he would have gotten the same or better deal much more easily.

Small courthouse, small case, it's true. But it doesn't matter. In any case. In any court. It's essential to know your judge, your courthouse, everyone in it, and everything else that might contribute to your success or failure for your client.

2. TELL YOUR STORY

As trial lawyers, we are storytellers. We tell the story about an impor-tant event in someone's life or business. I experienced this vividly in Hyattsville. Five days a week, fifty-plus cases a day, folks would line up and wait patiently to tell me their story. Some of them were short and simple, but others were much longer and more fully developed. I dis-covered that it mattered. Each story mattered in my consideration of the case. Each story mattered to that individual defendant. Each defendant had a different story, and each told their story differently. Often the story was just to get some sympathy, to lower the fine or the insurance points, and that was expected and OK. The law should honor differing circumstances, differing motivations, and differing lives. Some of the stories were much more involved, trying to explain what had happened and why, or trying to show that they had not violated the law or at least had not intended to.

I remember one woman in particular. She was there on a relatively minor traffic violation; I can't remember the details. It was something where a simple "I'm sorry" would have gotten her out of court quickly with a small fine. But she was determined to show us that she was in the right and therefore determined to go to trial. The police officer's testimony in my case was relatively straightforward and hard to contest, but in her case, she got up and made an extraordinary presentation. She told a detailed, sincere story, and brought maps, photos, charts, and all kinds of impressive materials to tell it with. She put them together carefully, respectfully, and thoughtfully.

When she was done, I looked first at the officer who had issued a citation to get his reaction. I never wanted to undercut the officers if I could avoid it. He smiled at me as if to say, it's OK, whatever you want to do is fine. No conviction, fine, or other punishment could make it so clear that she was treating this matter seriously and respectfully. After all, from the officer's perspective, wasn't that the point? Then I looked up at the magistrate, with the same unspoken question, and got the same unspoken reply.

So I moved to dismiss the charge. The judge first complimented the officer for his professionalism and testimony, then thanked me for doing a fine job trying to case, and finally turned to the defendant and thanked her for taking the matter so seriously, investing so much time and effort into her case and the trial, and giving such a clear indication that she understood the law and would not make the same mistake again. The defendant, shocked, burst into tears. She went over to the officer and shook hands, then shook my hand, and then thanked the magistrate and assured us all that it would never happen again. We were all quite confident that it wouldn't.

Her story, and those of the other fifty-plus cases a day, helped me to understand the importance of storytelling in court. This is real life, not legal fiction. Real life comes with details, emotions, and an interesting and hopefully compelling story.

3. DO THE RIGHT THING

Most of the crimes we dealt with in the Magistrate's Court were every-day ordinary crimes, often committed by everyday ordinary people. No serial killers, no inside traders, no corrupt politicians. Mostly people trying to live their lives, but doing it wrong, at least once. In that real-world environment, the magistrate's mantra, to himself and to everyone in the courthouse, was "Do the Right Thing."

Mom was clocked at 44 MPH in a 30-MPH zone. But if the letter mom brought in from the elementary school confirmed that the school had asked her to hurry, because her daughter had taken quite sick, and was in tears in the school nurse's office, shouldn't we take that into consideration?

There's no excuse for driving while impaired. But if dad lost his job that day, and stopped at a bar for the first time because he was too ashamed to go home, can't we listen to his loving family's pleas to not pile on too hard in this difficult time?

Was it the wisdom of Solomon? No, just common sense and caring. We processed a lot of cases, and many—maybe most—were pretty routine. But each one meant something to those involved and deserved our consideration. Some more urgently than others.

One day, a mother came in with her 15- or 16-year-old son who had been arrested for simple possession of marijuana in one of the parks in the area. Hardly the crime of the century, but in our early morning conference, the park ranger who made the arrest warned: "This kid is headed down the wrong path. I've seen him out there before, and he was nothing but arrogant and insulting when I arrested him." Sure enough, in court, when I got to him and Mom in line, that description held true: "This is bull _ _ _ _!" "You're an _ _ _ hole!" And with a final expletive, he stormed out of the courtroom, telling Mom to "Take care of this s _ _ _!"

At which point, Mom started to cry. She was losing her baby boy and didn't know how to fix it. Marijuana was one thing, but what would come next? She knew no way to steer him away from the tough, older crowd he was starting to hang out with. She loved her son deeply, but he had become just as arrogant and abusive at home as he was in court. She was out of options and desperate for help, wherever she could get it. I was an Assistant US Attorney, an honored position, surely I could do something to help her.

I had no idea what to do, so I ignored the line and went back into chambers to talk with the magistrate. He listened to my recitation, flipped through the thin file to familiarize himself with the facts, and said to me, "I'm going to come out on the bench early; call this case first."

So I did. I called the case. The judge had the arresting officer describe the offense, and then turned to the defendant and asked him what he had to say. There's no transcript, and it was a long time ago, but what followed remains pretty strong in my mind:

Defendant: This is a BS charge; it wasn't even my pot.

Judge: I would warn you not to say anything further without getting legal counsel.

Defendant: That's BS, I don't need a lawyer. I know my rights.

Judge: So, you understand what you're charged with?

Defendant: Yes, it's BS.

Judge: So, you understand what the penalties are for this offense?

Defendant: My mom is here; she'll pay the fine.

Judge: I asked you if you understand what the penalties are.

Defendant: Do I look like a lawyer?

Judge: Mr. Small, would you read into the record the statutory penalties for this offense?

Mr. Small: Yes, your honor. It's a maximum term of imprisonment of one year and a fine of $10,000.

Judge: Yes, that's correct. I find the defendant guilty as charged, and finding no remorse and the likelihood of a repeat offender, I hereby sentence you to the maximum one-year imprisonment and a $10,000 fine, to be paid by you, not your mother. You'll have plenty of time to think about what a smartass you are. Mr. US Marshal, please cuff him, step him back and put him in the holding cell.

Defendant: What?? You can't do that! What??

Judge: Mr. US Marshal, cuff him and put him in the holding cell.

At which point, the marshal grabbed him, cuffed him, and dragged him kicking, screaming, and crying back into the little holding cell we had, where he was chained to the bench and sat. And sat. And cried. Throughout the day, as we worked through other cases, the magistrate would occasionally call the marshal and me up to the bench and ask, "How's he doing?" The marshal reported that the defendant was crying and begging for help. "That's a start," the magistrate responded.

Finally, late in the afternoon, the magistrate called the mom and me up to the bench. He asked her what she wanted him to do. Mom, still in tears, thanked the magistrate for his toughness, and said that she was willing to try to take him home. So, the magistrate had him brought out, still in the prisoner's chains. The arrogant jerk of the morning was now a puddle of sobbing Jello, as a 15- or 16-year-old would be, after a day like that. The magistrate stepped in: "Young man, if you think a day in a holding cell was fun, perhaps you should try 365 days in a federal prison? Is that what you want?"

A:	"No, your honor, please. Please let me go, I'm so sorry!"

M:	"I'm inclined to sentence you to the full year. The only reason I'm reconsidering, the *only* reason, is that your mother seems like a good person, and she has asked me with all her heart to give you a second chance. Do you think that you deserve a second chance?

A:	Yes, your honor, please!

M:	Given your lousy attitude, I'm not so sure.

A:	*(sobs)* I'm really sorry! I didn't mean it! I'm really sorry!

M.	Well, *only* because I believe that your mother is a good person, and she has asked for mercy for you, I am willing to suspend your sentence. But let me make something very clear to you *(voice rising)*. Are you listening carefully?

A:	Yes, your honor.

M:	Are you listening very carefully *(voice rising)*?

A:	*(sobbing)* Yes, your honor.

M:	*(voice rising)* If I *ever, ever* see you in this courthouse again, or ever hear from your mother that you've screwed up again, you just pack your toothbrush because you are going to jail for the maximum. Do you understand me?

A:	Yes, your honor.

M:	Do you have any questions about what I've just told you?

A:	No, your honor! I'm so sorry. I won't do it again!

M:	You'd better not; now go home with your mother!

Mom took him out of the courtroom, led him to the bathroom so he could recover for a moment, and meanwhile rushed back into the courtroom, in tears again, gave me a hug, and said "Thank you, Thank you," then went up to the bench and said the same thing to the judge. "Good luck," he said, "Come back if we can help." And she left.

Under the unwritten rules of that court, a first offense simple possession charge without serious aggravating facts, would never have resulted in prison time. Never. But to the magistrate, that wasn't the point. Maybe the work of a wise experienced jurist and a brand new lawyer that day ended up not making any difference. But maybe, just maybe, it did. And it was our responsibility, in his mind, to try to do the right thing.

As trial lawyers, our obligation is to represent our clients zealously, but we should never forget that our clients, and everyone involved in the case, are real people with real problems. Whenever we can, within the bounds of representing our clients, we should always seek ways to, as the magistrate said, "Do the right thing!"

1

Grain Dust: Farmers Export
Galveston, TX

EXECUTIVE SUMMARY

Criminal trial of top managers of a grain elevator that exploded, killing 18 people.

As you read this chapter, be aware of:

- **Law as a force for change**: The law can be a powerful weapon. Wielded properly, it can create meaningful change.

- **Common ground**: Everything we do in a courtroom should mean something. Learn the rules of your court and judge, and find common ground to obey them, but to still try your case.

- **Strangers in a bar**: Prepare your case, and your witnesses, by telling the story to nonlawyers: family, friends, strangers in a bar. Then listen to their questions and concerns. Those will likely be the jury's concerns, as well.

- **Captain of the ship**: Don't cede control of your case to your experts. Understand what they have to say, challenge it, then work out the best way to present it.

- **Prior inconsistent statement**: When you have a prior inconsistent statement, just relax and remember the "Three Cs": commit, credit, confront.

- **Feedback is like gold**: Seek out feedback on your trials wherever you can find it: Colleagues, observers, and participants.

GRAIN DUST

Grain dust is a funny thing. What could be more innocent than grain? No one worries about a loaf of bread falling on them or exploding in the bread aisle of the supermarket. Grain dust is a natural byproduct of moving grain. Sure enough, in a pile on the ground, you can put a blow torch to it and not much will happen. But stir up that pile so it is suspended in the air, like a cloud, and an amazing thing happens: it transforms into something that is highly explosive. Indeed, grain dust suspended in the air can be four times *more* explosive than coal dust. So, the obvious answer is to keep it on the ground and to keep the ground clean. Seems pretty simple. It's not.

Across the Midwest, the big, mechanized combines work day and night to harvest the grain. One acre can yield more than forty-six bushels of wheat, weighing about sixty pounds per bushel. The farm trucks bring it to a local grain elevator to hold until the next train comes in. In that train, each railcar can carry almost 200,000 pounds of grain, representing the product of almost seventy acres of farmland. As a train gathers railcars from different local grain elevators, it often stretches to more than 100 cars, heading to the southern ports. When they get there, and reach one of the huge export grain elevators, each railcar is unloaded at the Rail Dump, with the grain then usually traveling by conveyer belt through an underground tunnel to the base of the elevator and carried up into the elevator to hold until the next cargo ship comes in, to be loaded with grain for export around the world.

At each step along the way, from harvest to export, as the grain kernels rub together, it produces grain dust. The further along the way, the more grain, the more dust. When a railcar is opened and quickly dumps its 200,000 pounds, it can produce a small cloud of grain dust in the rail dump. By the time all 100 railcars in that long train are dumped, that's a lot of clouds.

You have to be careful to avoid sparks, of course, but you also have to keep the grain elevator clean. Constantly. Meticulously. Because if, God forbid, a spark ignites the cloud of grain dust from dumping a single railcar, it can cause an explosion, but hopefully a minor one that goes nowhere. If the elevator is dirty, with piles of grain dust everywhere, that initial explosion can stir up and ignite the next pile, and the next pile, and begin a chain reaction explosion that can continue for as long as there are more piles of grain dust to feed it.

Grain elevators today use various mechanical and technological devices to help keep things clean, but not so long ago, they relied in large part on crews of workers with brooms. That meant managers had to take laborers away from the all-important task of dumping more railcars to meet their company quotas. It didn't always work.

On Thursday, December 22, 1977, the huge Continental Grain Elevator in the port of Westwego, Louisiana, exploded, killing thirty-six people. The explosion traveled up the twenty-five-story concrete tower, which came crashing down on the administration building, where workers were celebrating the holidays. There were, literally, not enough workers left alive to confirm the exact cause and the responsibility for this tragedy. It's hard to build an investigation without witnesses.

Five days later, the Farmers Export grain elevator in the Port of Galveston, Texas, blew up. The explosion began in the rail dump, traveled 250 feet along an underground conveyor belt, and blew the roof off the twenty-story reinforced concrete tower. Eighteen workers were killed. All from exploding grain dust. This time, there were some survivors and other sources to aid an investigation.

THE LAW AS A FORCE FOR CHANGE

Murder is wrong. Everybody knows that. It's one of the Ten Commandments. It's a crime and always has been. But other things that may be wrong have not always been so clearly viewed as criminal. White Collar Crime is a relatively recent vintage. Until fairly recently, the common view was that "criminals" were ruffians, not men in suits and ties. Nonviolent or victimless (in the direct sense) actions were hard for many to accept as crimes.

Health and safety was one of the slowest areas to change. Traditionally, if a health and safety case made it to court at all, it was as a civil lawsuit, either by the government or injured victims, and brought against the corporate entity responsible. In most instances, that really meant the entity's insurance company. After all, it was just about money.

One result was that the managers on the ground, the people who were most likely to have seen—or even directed—the problem, and who were most likely to be able to keep it from happening again, were several layers away from any litigation. In the months or years it takes a case to wind through the system, the managers on the ground had been back hard at work, and the incident or issue was a distant memory. As a force for change, it often was too remote.

In 1970, there was a major shift. Congress created the Occupational Safety and Health Administration (OSHA), and that law included criminal penalties against individuals for serious violations that caused death. That meant jail, not a distant insurer. There were few cases brought, and most federal prosecutors didn't even know the law existed. It was too new, too different.

Ten years later, the Department of Justice (DOJ) decided that the law was on the books for a reason, and it should be used in appropriate serious cases. But how to convince busy prosecutors around the country to add this new law and concept to their burdens? The DOJ's Criminal Division decided to create a unit of attorneys specializing in health and safety cases based in Washington, DC, but traveling everywhere to offer support and encouragement to local prosecutors to bring criminal health and safety cases. One year out of law school, I became a part of that unit.

Almost every case we brought was a shock to the defendants and people in similar positions elsewhere. That's not the way it had worked. Criminal? OK, maybe someone screwed up. Maybe they could have been more careful. It was a shame that someone died as a result. But no one *intended* to kill them; is that really criminal? The DOJ wanted to get people's attention. In many cases, it worked.

So, when fifty-four people died within five days in the two grain dust explosions, OSHA came to the DOJ and said, "We have a problem in the grain elevator business, and whatever we're doing isn't enough." The DOJ and the US Attorney's Office in Houston agreed to open a grand jury investigation, with our little unit providing support. Dick Tallman, a fellow member of the unit, started the ball rolling, then passed it to me when he left. The investigation itself was a shock to the industry: grain elevator employees and managers, company executives, and government regulators being summoned to testify before a federal grand jury and questioned by DOJ attorneys. But the real shock came when the two top managers of the Farmers Export grain elevators were indicted—individually—for criminal violations of the OSHA Act, with potential penalties including fines and jail on each count. The world had changed. It was time—long past time for the fifty-four dead—to look at health and safety in the grain industry in a whole new light.

"Ready for Trial?"

As one of the first high-profile criminal OSHA prosecutions, the Farmers Export case drew a great deal of attention in the media, the industry, and the legal community. Both defendants retained experienced trial counsel, former US Attorneys. Both had second-chair lawyers assisting them who were older and more experienced than me. I was excited to be part of the case, carrying the bags and doing the research for the lead counsel. I could learn a lot by watching such experienced trial lawyers.

The case was brought in Galveston, where there was a small federal courthouse—basically one judge, one of everything. Judge Gibson was a very experienced and very strict judge. At the time, there was no US Attorney's Office in Galveston, so prosecutors would have to drive the 50 miles from Houston or stay in a hotel in Galveston. The Chief of the Criminal Division in the Houston US Attorney's Office was going to try the case for the government. He was a very experienced trial lawyer, which was necessary for such a complex and challenging case. We began to prepare for trial.

Every case has surprises and unexpected hurdles. Our first one came just a couple of weeks before the trial date. The Chief of the Criminal Division had a conflict. I don't remember what it was, but he couldn't try the case on the scheduled date. No problem, I said, we'll get a continuance. Oh no, I was told, that's not how things work in Galveston. Judge Gibson runs his calendar very strictly and doesn't care much about individual government attorneys' schedules, when presumably there are always more who can step in. He doesn't give continuances, and when he says, "Ready for trial?", it's not really a question, it's an order. The case is going to trial as scheduled.

I reminded the chief how important this case was to the DOJ, to OSHA, and to families of the deceased, and how embarrassing it would be to not have experienced lead counsel. All this said with just a bit of panic. All was well, he assured me. One of the most experienced and talented trial lawyers in his office happened to be down in Galveston trying a case, and George had agreed to step in for the chief. Reassured, I headed down to Galveston, checked into the government-rate hotel, and went to the courthouse to meet George.

The chief's description was accurate: George was a great guy and a great lawyer. But when I finally met with him after his long trial day, something had got lost in the communications. What the chief did not tell me—or didn't understand—was that George was in the middle of trying—solo—a complex multiple-defendant drug case. What's more, the case was taking longer than expected—much to Judge Gibson's dismay—so the judge was holding them to long trial days and had announced that he would start the Farmers Export trial as soon as the jury went out to deliberate in the drug trial.

"Dan, this sounds like an interesting case," George said, "and I look forward to working with you! I'll have to take the first few days of your trial to learn about the case, but once I'm up to speed, I'll be happy to try to help you any way you tell me!" Help me? Help ME? The ripples of panic I had felt talking with the chief became a tidal wave. George, I said, I'm just here to help *you*. I'm two years out of law school, I've never tried a major case before; I have no idea what I'm doing. Both defense counsels have second chairs with more experience than me! This is crazy.

George was surprised but far too seasoned a trial lawyer to let surprises worry him: "You're a bright guy, you'll do fine. I'll help you when I can. Besides, we don't have any choice, Judge Gibson doesn't give continuances. We're going to trial, do your best." I called my bosses in Washington, still in a state of panic, but when I described the situation, they agreed with George: "We're going to trial, do your best." So, I went to the little office in the Galveston courthouse reserved for prosecutors and started getting ready for trial. A couple days later, Judge Gibson interrupted the drug trial just long enough to hold a final pretrial conference in our case. When he looked at me and said "Ready for trial?", I understood that there was only one response: "Your Honor, the Government will be ready." Just have to step up and do our best.

FORMS OF EXPRESSION

Everything we do in a courtroom should mean something. How you speak, how you act, how you move, how you ask questions. None of this should be random; it should all have purpose and meaning. Giving an opening statement in the Farmers Export trial where eighteen people were dead, questioning workers who were themselves questioning why so many friends died and they did not, questioning the coroner on how the manner of the 18 deaths showed the direction and force of the explosion, how do you hold yourself, express yourself, in these types of situations? It was a real challenge.

Layer on top of that one of the basic conflicts of a trial. The lawyer is trying the case and wants to be in control of the courtroom. Ultimately, though, the judge controls the courtroom, to whatever extent they see fit. Of course, judges vary widely. Some will largely sit back and "let the lawyers try their case." Some exercise tight control at every step. Some are in the middle. So a trial lawyer has to know their judge, and understand and adapt to different courtroom environments. I learned this lesson the second day of trial.

I was questioning a witness on direct examination from the podium and realized that I needed a document from my table. I walked the couple steps to the table, picked up the document, and continued questioning the witness, with the document in one hand, and the other hand resting on the table. I had a nice rhythm going. Perhaps I could learn this trial thing after all, despite my panic?

"Bam!" Judge Gibson pounded his gavel so loudly it shocked everyone. "Sidebar!" he said angrily. And I knew it was over: two days into my first big trial, and I had already screwed it up somehow. I didn't know how, but clearly the case I cared about was lost and I would be fired from the job I loved. Perhaps I could go back to bartending. All that and more went through my head as I slowly walked up to the sidebar.

"Mr. Small," Judge Gibson said sternly at the sidebar, "I know you haven't tried many cases in this district." (Actually, I hadn't tried many cases in **any** district.) "But we don't *lean* in my courtroom! You will stand up straight, behind the podium!" "Yes, Your Honor," I mumbled and stood there frozen at sidebar. What happens next? Handcuffs? Directed verdict? Contempt citation? As I didn't say or do anything else, we stood there awkwardly for a bit, and Judge Gibson finally gave me an odd look, and said, "That is all." That is all? Really? No three words have ever given me greater joy. The case was not lost. I had survived the pounding of the gavel, lived to fight another day. I needed to learn from this traumatic experience.

And so, I adapted. I learned to blend expression with control. At first, I kept both hands gripping the podium and mumbled my questions robotically. But then just one hand. Then no hands, moving for emphasis, just keeping behind the podium. I realized that the podium still allowed for endless forms of expression: in tone, in volume, in pace, the works. Indeed, it added one more prop to the show. There were plenty more loud gavels during the month-long trial, but none related to the podium. Judge Gibson and I had reached common ground: I would respect his rule about staying behind the podium, and he would let me try my case.

Trials are a constant search for common ground: with the judge, the jury, the witness, and even opposing counsel. Two days into my first big trial, wise old Judge Gibson taught me that lesson, and I will be forever grateful.

FIVE TIMES MORE EXPLOSIVE
THAN COAL DUST

My favorite quote about expert witnesses comes from the *Kerstetter* case, more than 60 years ago: "Expert opinion . . . is only an ordinary guess, in evening clothes."[1] If that's true, we lawyers have to fit the clothes just right. We have to determine what our core themes are and how our experts can help convey them. When it comes to experts, the lawyer remains the captain of the ship. Not always easy: these witnesses are, after all, "experts," and a good expert can do a lot to help guide the ship. But we are the trial lawyer. It's our case: we know what we want, what we need, and what's going to happen. And we're responsible if we don't exercise that control.

Experts were a key part of the Farmers Export trial, but at the time, the science of grain dust was still evolving, and there weren't that many real experts. To begin, I tried to read everything I could find on the subject. I wanted to be as expert as the experts, and I needed to understand how to present this to a jury.

I spent a good deal of time preparing my expert witness on the second point: presenting to a jury. I'm a big believer that one of the most important tools for preparing your case—any case—is to tell the story to nonlawyers: family, friends, and strangers at a bar and listen to their reactions and questions. That's your jury—not fellow lawyers—listen to them!

When I did this, one of the things I kept hearing was: "Grain dust?" "Huh?" "Explosive?" Our expert could *say* that grain dust was four times

---

[1] E. M. Kerstetter, Inc. v. Com, 404 Pa. 168, 171 A.2d 163 (Pa. 1961).

more explosive than coal dust, but the jury needed more. To them, grain was just bread or breakfast cereal. They needed to see and feel this strange transformation. It needed to be part of their basic understanding of the world, not just fancy words from some paid expert.

I told my expert that before we got into all the science and details, we needed a basic demonstration. Even back then, pre-9/11, we couldn't blow anything up in the courtroom, so we did it in the parking lot behind the courthouse and videotaped it. My expert took one pile of grain dust and split it into two piles. He lit a blowtorch and put it on the first pile: not much happened, just sizzled. Then he put the second pile into a clear plexiglass box he had built with two additions: a foot pump to send a burst of air into the box to stir up the pile, and a spark igniter. He stepped on the pump, the grain dust was suspended in the air, lit the spark, and POW! Loud dramatic explosion from a small pile of grain dust! We were all shocked. Now he could take the stand and explain how and why it was explosive, but the jury already understood and accepted the basic truth.

With almost any expert, think about what your core theme is ("Four times more explosive than coal dust"), and be creative about simple demonstrations or other things you can do to help the jury truly accept and believe that core theme. Let them carry that with them throughout the trial. I'm confident that every juror had the surprise of that explosion front and center in their minds throughout the trial.

EXPERT WITNESSES: KNOW YOUR CASE

The captain of the ship also has to prepare for stormy weather. But if you haven't become as expert as your expert, how can you understand what's coming or prepare them for it? The defense also found a grain industry/grain dust expert. He was not as qualified as our expert but very smooth. On direct examination, he gave defense counsel a surprisingly brief but neatly packaged presentation. A little voice in the back of my head kept saying, "too brief" and "too smooth." What to do?

The late, great Irving Younger's *Ten Commandments of Cross Examination* are filled with warnings against winging it on cross: Don't ask a question you don't know the answer to—Don't ask open questions—Don't let the witness explain—Don't ask the one question too many.

I had heard his wonderful lecture (you can and should find it online). I knew the horror stories of lawyers far more experienced than me who had violated the Commandments. But there was that insistent voice in my head: "too smooth."

Trials often come down to a tough call between following the rules and following your instincts. Most of the time, following the rules is the safer course. Maybe I was just too young and stupid to follow the rules. Maybe I was just lucky. It certainly wasn't experience or wisdom. They say that the Good Lord looks out for children and other fools. So, using the knowledge I had accumulated in my studies, I started lobbing questions at their expert. Open questions, leading questions, all kinds of questions testing his knowledge.

The first couple of questions were disastrous, and a wiser man would have stopped there: They just gave him the opportunity to repeat parts of his nice presentation from direct, which he did, almost word for word. But surprisingly, the little voice in my head didn't say, "Sorry, I blew it; sit down before this gets worse!" Instead, it said, "Listen! Use your ears! Just like I told you: too smooth!" So, I threw out another question and got another rewind of the direct exam presentation. And then it hit me: That's all there was! This witness's expertise was only an inch deep, and he had to put everything he knew into his smooth, little, direct presentation. There was nothing behind it. No one who knew the subject matter on the other side had prepared him or questioned him to see how he would do on cross-examination.

I went on for another hour or more, peppering him with questions. Demanding details, support, explanations, backup, and things a good expert would have killed me on. I had never cross-examined an expert witness before: what the heck did I know? But it seemed to be the right thing to do, and with this witness, it worked. Slowly but surely, everyone in the courtroom realized that they'd been conned: the smooth presentation was just a front, there was nothing behind the curtain. Through no particular skill of mine, the witness was pretty much destroyed. He left the stand and his name was never spoken again, even in the defense closing, All because of that little voice. Listen, listen, listen: to your instincts, to the testimony, to what the jury is really hearing. Then follow the rules. Well, most of the time. You are a trial lawyer. Know your case. And if you know your case, believe in yourself.

COMMIT, CREDIT, CONFRONT!

There are many ways to attack a witness's credibility. Opportunity to observe: was it too far or too dark for the witness to see? Bias: does the witness have a prior history—good or bad—with one of the parties? Self-interest: does the witness have an interest in the outcome of the case? Character: has the witness been convicted of crimes? Contradictory evidence: are there documents or other evidence that contradict the witness's story? And lots more.

One of the classic challenges to a witness's credibility is the prior inconsistent statement. Somewhere along the way, the witness has said something—in a statement, deposition, tape, wherever—that contradicts their testimony. One of the keys to successful witness preparation is making sure you have found any prior statements and preparing the witness to deal with any inconsistencies. One of the keys to successful cross-examination is knowing how to effectively use the prior inconsistent statement. For that purpose, I learned from great lawyers and great teachers who look to the "Three Cs."

The "Three Cs" for prior inconsistent statements are, "commit, credit, confront."

> **Commit** the witness to the current statement ("On direct exam, your story was that . . .").
>
> **Credit** the prior statement ("You had time to prepare for deposition with your lawyer; you took an oath, just like you did here; you knew how important it was to tell the truth; you had a chance to review your testimony and submit any changes; etc.").
>
> **Confront** with the contradiction ("So, in your story today, you said the light was green, but in your sworn deposition you said it was red!").

In the Farmers Export grain elevator explosion trial, the defense started off claiming they had done nothing wrong. But as witness after witness talked about how dirty the elevator was, with piles of grain dust everywhere, and how management was pushing so hard to dump railcars faster that sparks were flying, they fell back to two other lines of defense: First, "Okay, but they're not **criminals**, they didn't intend to hurt anyone." Second, "This is really just a dispute between labor and management."

To some extent, that's how it appeared. The laborer witnesses talked about how bad things were and how little management cared about safety. The management witnesses talked about how clean it was and how safety was their highest priority. So, imagine the defense counsel's delight when they found a witness who bridged that gap. Billy, we'll call him, had been a laborer at the time of the explosion, but had since been promoted to management and now supported management's story all the way.

I don't have the transcript or exhibits (the case was never appealed), so all this is from rough memory, but basically Billy testified on direct that:

- Management was very conscientious.
- Cleaning crews were sweeping the elevator regularly.
- The elevator was so clean, you could eat off the floors.
- Safety was the highest priority.
- They were very careful in the rail dump.

He knew most of the eighteen dead and was sorry for their loss, but it was an accident.

On the night of the explosion, OSHA Investigator Don Donnelly happened to be driving in Galveston and heard about the blast on his police scanner radio. He raced to the chaotic scene with the first responders and immediately started interviewing witnesses. Don was a great investigator and a great guy. I think of him fondly in the style of the old TV detective Colombo, played so well by Peter Falk: disheveled, rumpled, and unassuming, but smart and effective. He's the kind of person that people opened up to easily, talked to openly, and then forgot.

That night, Don had in his car a pad of simple one-page interview forms. At the top, after the witness's name, it said something like, "I voluntarily and willingly make this true statement." The middle had space for Don to write up a brief statement. Then at the bottom, above the witness's signature, it said: "I have carefully reviewed the above statement and it is true and accurate. Signed under pains and penalties of perjury." Short and sweet.

So, you know where this is going, right? On that chaotic night of the explosion, Investigator Donnelly had interviewed Billy and had him sign a statement. Billy had long since forgotten. I had actually considered calling Billy as a government witness (which would have required me to disclose his statement), but I was told that he had gone over to the dark side, so I didn't call him. When I saw his name on the defense witness list, I searched my soul, and more than a few law books, about whether I had to turn over his statement. In a criminal case like this, if someone is a defense witness, the government is generally not obligated to turn over that witness's statement unless it is exculpatory—which this certainly was not.

So I didn't turn it over. I had Investigator Donnelly sit in the middle of the crowded courtroom before Billy appeared so he wouldn't stick out too much, kept the statement buried in my file, and waited for the cross-examination. Nervous? No, I was scared to death. Lawyers can go through a whole career without being handed a set-up like this. Handed through no work of my own. Here I was, two years out of law school, and scared that I didn't know what I was doing and would blow this opportunity, and with it, my case. All I could think of as I sat there waiting was those three words, "commit, credit, confront!"

Again, no transcript or exhibits exist, but here's my memory, in much condensed form.

I. COMMIT
    A. Testified for company
        a) You are now part of management
        b) Met with company counsel before
    B. Story today:
        a) Management was conscientious
        b) Safety was highest priority
        c) Cleaning crews swept Grain Elevator regularly
        d) GE was clean
            • You could eat off the floor

II. CREDIT
    A. Remember night of explosion
        a) Rescue workers, firefighters, investigators
    B. Key part of any investigation:
        a) Interviewing witnesses
        b) Important for witnesses to tell truth

   C. *Did you* lie to investigator that night?

   D. *Would you* lie to investigator that night?

   E. OSHA Investigator

      a) Interviewed witnesses

         • Asked witnesses to sign statement

         • Have record of the truth

      b) **Recognize** S.A. Donnelly? *NO?*

         • Spoke night of explosion

         • Wrote down what you said

         • Asked you to read it carefully? *YOU DON'T REMEMBER?*

   F. Exhibit. 35—Recognize your signature? *YES?*

      a) Oath like here.

      b) Sworn Statement. "True and Correct"

      c) Knew how important it was to tell the truth

III. CONFRONT

Story for Company	Sworn Statement That Night
Management was conscientious	"All management cared about was making their quotas"
Cleaning crews swept the elevator regularly	"Crews taken off cleaning to dump more railcars"
Elevator was clean; you could eat off the floor	"Piles of grain dust everywhere"
Safety was highest priority	"Competition between shifts to dump most railcars"
	"Sparks flying as railcars banged together"

It was an amazing experience. Billy was totally caught off guard and totally flummoxed. By the end, if I had said, "And isn't it true that the moon is made of green cheese?", he probably would have said, "Yes, Mr. Small, if that's in my statement." Defense counsel tried a couple of random objections but could do nothing to stop the train wreck that their much-heralded bridge witness had turned into. And all of it not from any particular skill of mine, but from lessons learned from others: "commit, credit, confront."

THE VALUE OF FEEDBACK

Trials are such great live drama, it amazes me that so often they go forward without an audience. Oh, sure, some celebrity trials are on TV, but those are often poor examples, and watching bits and pieces on TV is no match for watching the real thing live. I wish more people understood what they're missing. And what a wasted opportunity for trial lawyers: to not receive feedback from the audience. What better way to learn?

When I moved back from Washington, DC, to Boston to join the US Attorney's Office Public Corruption Unit, there was a great group of about a dozen retired gentlemen who had discovered the Boston federal courthouse as a source of endless fascination. They would gather early every morning in the courthouse cafeteria for breakfast (remember when cafeteria breakfasts were delicious and cheap? They were.). There, they would review the court's published daily docket for all the judges, see what looked interesting, split up among the different courtrooms, and go watch. At the lunch break, they would reconvene in the cafeteria (delicious and cheap lunch!) and compare notes on what they had seen in the different trials. Over time, they had become expert observers and critiquers of trial practice. I befriended them, and they became an enjoyable and invaluable resource. They would tell me stories on what was going right and wrong in other trials. But it was when I was in trial that they were most valuable. "How did I do?" I would ask. And they would tell me straight out. Nothing escaped them:

- "Mr. Small, Juror #6 doesn't believe this witness, hit him hard."
- "Mr. Small, maybe you should focus more on X than Y?"
- "Mr. Small, you need to do more to explain how this worked."
- "Mr. Small, in your closing argument, be sure to focus on . . ."

There is no way to put a value on what I learned from these fine gentlemen, both for individual trials and generally as a developing trial lawyer.

But I already knew the value of feedback from experienced observers. I learned it in the Farmers Export trial. Think about a small courthouse: one judge, one clerk, one court reporter. When they get together, as they did regularly, for lunch, drinks, or just during the many lulls in the normal day, what do they talk about? OK, maybe sports, politics, fishing, whatever. But eventually, they talk about what they've been watching all day: trials. So, over time, the three of them became a committee of expert trial critiquers but often with no one else to provide the critique to! What a waste!

After a month of trial, no one expected the Farmers Export jury to come back with a verdict quickly. Yet there was nothing to do, nowhere to go. They could come back with a question or something at any moment. Nervous and bored, I wandered the halls of the small courthouse. At one point, I walked past the door to the small, one-room library, and much to my surprise, heard voices inside. In all my time in that court-house, I had never seen or heard anyone else in the library. Curious, I opened the door.

Two years out of law school, certain basic principles were fresh in my brain. A big one was *ex parte*: a party should not have contact with the court without the other party present. So, when I opened the door to the library, I was horrified to find the judge, clerk, and court reporter gathering around the old library table with a deck of cards and a bottle of amber liquid, passing the time. My law school instincts said "run!" so I started to close the door. But too late: Judge Gibson called out, "Mr. Small, come on in, pull up a chair!" Law school had also taught me, "When a federal judge issues an order, you have to comply!" So now, two basic law school teachings were in direct conflict. What to do? Which principle prevailed? Nothing in law school had prepared me for this. With great trepidation, I opened the door the rest of the way, went inside, and pulled up a chair.

What followed was nothing short of incredible. For the next four hours, this panel of expert trial-watchers walked through the entire month-long trial, step by step, and gave me feedback on virtually everything I had done. This was before we had ready access online to everyone's background, so I'm not sure they fully appreciated how totally inexperienced I was, but they suspected: "We were worried about you at first, but you came on strong as the trial went on!"

Everything I had done came under scrutiny, with constructive ideas about how to do it better. The things I had done well (the defense expert, the cross of Billy) came in for praise, but they were unsparing in critiquing things I could improve ("let's talk about your opening.") I had worked multiple jobs and gone into debt to go to law school, but the truth is, I learned more about trials in those four hours than I did in three years of law school. And those three gentlemen didn't charge me a dime: I drank their amber liquid and broke even at cards. And I will never forget those four hours around an old library table. What we do as trial lawyers is important and challenging. We need to seek out—and value—feedback wherever it comes from. I owe debts of gratitude that I can never repay, whether to those 12 retired gentlemen in the Boston cafeteria or to the library table committee in Galveston.

All I can do is try to pay it forward, as they did, as we all should, to other fledging trial lawyers, and hope that my advice helps.

"How Do You Define Success?"

We try cases to win. That's clear. We are competitive by nature and would have it no other way. But every case is different, and sometimes it's hard not to wonder what it is we have really accomplished by winning. How do we define success? Did I really change anything today or make a difference? Tough questions.

OSHA asked the DOJ to prosecute the Farmers Export case because they saw a problem in the grain elevator business that they had been unable to fix and hoped that we could make a difference. Fifty-four people had died in two explosions in five days. Something needed to change. Minds needed to change. Something dramatic had to get the grain industry's attention. Maybe prosecuting these two individual managers criminally would help. I was sent down from Washington, DC, to assist and show the flag. Everyone understood that this was not an ordinary or routine case. There was more at stake.

In the beginning, the defense took the high road: it's important to everyone that grain moves from the farms to hungry people overseas quickly and efficiently. It's a challenging job, but these men did it well. Safety was a high priority, and no one ever thought something like this would happen. But much of the evidence painted a different picture: The grain elevator was a mess with piles of grain dust everywhere. They had taken the crews off sweeping and moved them to the rail dump to help meet their corporate quotas for dumping railcars. To encourage this, management had set up a competition between the shifts to see who could dump the most railcars, promising a pizza party for the winning shift. The crews were banging railcars together to move them faster and sparks were flying. There was no pizza offered for safety. It was a disaster waiting to happen, our expert said.

So, the lawyers retreated to another line of defense. OK, maybe they screwed up, maybe they should have done more. But they are not "criminals," not muggers or rapists, they didn't intend to kill anyone. Clearly, the law did not require us to prove that they intended to kill anyone: that would have been murder, a different issue. But views on white-collar crime had not developed as far then as they have in the years since. Today, most jurors would say, "so what?" and follow the law. Back then, the idea of men in suits and ties being criminals was still fairly unusual, and so "they're not criminals," struck a chord with some jurors.

Throughout a month-long trial, the jury was generally very attentive, clearly upset about the deaths, but tough to read on the bigger issue. Some of the evidence was hard to hear: workers in tears about the deaths of their friends and co-workers and angry that management hadn't done more to prevent it; the coroner using the manner of deaths to show the force and weight of the explosion; investigators describing the chaos and devastation. And every night, I'd go back to my government-rate hotel room and wonder what the jury was thinking.

After the close of the evidence, closing arguments, and legal instructions from the judge, the jury went out to deliberate. It felt like forever—then and now in my memory—but I think it was four days. Finally, it became clear that they could not reach a unanimous verdict. What we heard was that they were unanimous in agreeing that the two managers had done wrong. But three of the eleven could not make the next step, to call these nice respectable men "criminals." So, the jury was deadlocked, 8-3 for conviction. Judge Gibson had to call a mistrial.

There it was: all that hard work and a difficult month of trial, and all we got was a hung jury. Winning is the goal of every trial, and by that measure we had failed. Dejected, I wandered around the courthouse, spent some time in a local bar I had come to like, packed up my stuff, and headed back to my office in Washington, DC. Not an easy time.

But then a remarkable thing started to happen. When a jury is deadlocked, and the judge declares a mistrial because, without a unanimous verdict, the trial essentially cannot conclude, the government then generally has the option to retry the case. To start over and do it again. To make that tough decision, the two main questions are usually:

1. What could we do differently, or better, in a second trial, that might lead to a different result?
2. What would be the purpose of a retrial, what would we accomplish?

Sometimes, the answers are very clear, for example:

1. Witness X screwed up badly. If we retry the case without him, using other witnesses instead, it would be much better.
2. This is a serious violent criminal, we cannot let him get away with this, we have no choice.

The answers in the Farmers Export case were different. On the first question, it was very flattering to me. The consensus was that, despite my inexperience, the evidence had largely come in as we wanted it, there were no glaring errors, and no major strategy changes that might lead to a different result. In short, there was no reason to believe that a retrial would go better, and it might even be tougher, since the defense now knew our whole case. All this was nice to hear, but it was on the second question that things turned in an extraordinary way.

From all kinds of sources—our Investigator Don Donnelly, other OSHA investigators and administrators, people in the grain industry, and elsewhere—we were told: hung jury or not, our message had been heard. No one saw a month-long criminal trial and an 8-3 vote for conviction as vindication for the two executives or the rest of the industry. They saw it as a clear shot across the bow to the industry: "clean up your act." While I was bemoaning my "loss" (or at least failure to win), others were seeing it very differently. It took a while to understand.

So in the end, the DOJ, with OSHA's agreement, decided not to retry the case. There was no reason to believe that a second trial would go significantly better, and more important, to the extent that part of our purpose was to send a message, to be a force for change, we had "won." And it worked. By God, it worked. OSHA told us that grain elevators around the country started to change their practices, change their attitudes, and be a whole lot more responsive when OSHA walked in the door. I don't keep the statistics, so don't sue me if there's an outlier somewhere, but I was told that after fifty-four workers died in two explosions in five days that terrible December, there was not another multiple-death explosion in a grain elevator for at least ten years.

Ten years! Win/lose, succeed/fail. In every case, we need to think about what these words mean to us. What are we looking to accomplish? Sometimes, the definitions are easy, but don't be too fast to judge. All I know is that the Farmers Export trial, one of my biggest "failures" in the sense of not winning, will always be one of my proudest victories. Lessons learned.

2

Appling County

EXECUTIVE SUMMARY

From an eighteen- defendant drugs and corruption Racketeer Influenced and Corrupt Organizations Act (RICO) case in South Georgia. As you read this chapter, be aware of:

- **Law as a force for change:** When the facts and circumstances call for it, sometimes trial lawyers need to be creative and aggressive with the law.

- **Don't make promises you can't keep:** Before you make promises to the jury, in your opening or elsewhere, make sure you are confident and comfortable that the evidence will allow you to keep those promises.

- **Bring Out The Bad Stuff (BOBS):** Every witness has flaws. Work to develop trust with your witness, push to bring out those flaws, and then work together on how to present them. What you don't know will hurt you.

- **The wisdom of jurors:** Understand that jurors listen not just for the facts but also for justice. Develop and present your case to help guide them to do what's right, in your favor.

In the early days of the "War on Drugs," Florida was the focus, which made sense. With its 1,350 miles of coastline (not counting all the islands) and close proximity to the Caribbean and Central and South American sources of supply, it was a natural entry point. Law enforcement agencies of all shapes and sizes—local, county, state, and federal—all got money to try to cut off the supply of drugs coming into the United States through Florida.

The basic laws of supply and demand came into play. Those laws say that if you limit supply, without cutting off demand, several things may happen. First, the price will go up. Second, the market will seek other sources of supply. Both those things happened. The prices—and thus the potential profits for smugglers—went up. And smugglers looked for other locations that didn't have Florida's law enforcement pressure. One of those was right next door in Georgia.

Appling County is a small rural county in Southeast Georgia. Founded in 1818 and named after Lieutenant Colonel Daniel Appling, a soldier in the War of 1812, it's 512 square miles of mostly woods and farmland. The 1990 census figures gave this area a population of about 15,000 with a low average income, so drug profits were attractive. It was the perfect, out-of-the-way place. In the southern part of the county, well away from the county seat of Baxley, the Morris brothers owned the largest dairy farm in Georgia.

Two local men, Larry Jackson and Lemuel Morris, built an airstrip on the farm and started bringing in planeloads of drugs. They were careful. Among other things, they would often do it on a Friday night because everyone else in the county was way up in Baxley, or elsewhere, for Friday night high school football. They'd even talk about the different loads by using the name of the opposing team that particular night. They had a good thing going.

PLANTING THE SEEDS OF CORRUPTION

In Florida, corruption was a frequent companion to the drug trade, but it could be complicated. There were many overlapping agencies and jurisdictions. If you bribed a city cop to protect your drug business, the county, state, or federal agencies might still be all over you. In South Georgia, at that time, it was simpler. The county sheriff was a powerful figure who controlled most law enforcement in the county, and in some instances, pretty much controlled the county.

Of course, in a county as small as Appling, Jackson and Morris had grown up with the sheriff and his deputies, so reaching out to them was easy. They recruited and bribed the former sheriff, "Red" Carter, and the current sheriff, Joe Lightsey, who was then responsible for recruiting his deputies and others and paying them their share. It was surprisingly easy.

Too easy. The dollar numbers made it so. In one tape recording (more on that later), one of the deputy sheriffs tells Larry Jackson that he's worried about our pending investigation. To reassure him, Jackson asks what his annual salary is as a deputy, and then laughingly compares it to what the deputy made in the last six months just sitting around keeping an eye out for one evening a week. Both numbers were absurd and embarrassing: his pay is offensively low, and his cut for one evening protecting a planeload of drugs is irresistibly high.

When we eventually confronted one of the deputies and convinced him to plead guilty and cooperate (thus the tape recordings), he felt terrible about what he had done, but confused about how someone was supposed to put their life on the line as a cop, and also support a family, on such an absurdly low salary, when lowlifes are making more money in one night. They are not easy arguments to counter and are common throughout the "War on Drugs." We had to demonstrate that there were other consequences.

"YOU HAVE TO SAVE MY COUNTY!"

Secrets are hard to keep in a small town or county but they can easily tear it apart. Appling County became badly divided between those who didn't want drug smuggling and other illegal activities in their county, and those who supported the sheriff and either didn't believe or didn't care about the rumors of illegality. Slowly but surely, the rule of law was melting away. But what could be done about it? The sheriff was, in many respects, the most powerful elected official in the county.

Lewis Parker had grown up in Appling County in a family that had been there for generations and had considerable acreage in farmland, pecan orchards, and other uses. He didn't need the job. But when his complaints to the sheriff were ignored and suspicions of illegal activity grew, he decided that someone had to run against the sheriff. Lewis was not a law enforcement officer by profession. It's said that his "training" included watching the movie "Walking Tall" three times, starring the tough but honest sheriff with a Bible in one hand and a big stick in the other.

So he ran for sheriff. And he won. But just barely. The balance of power hung precariously in the balance. If Lewis didn't get things done, if the allegations swirling around the county weren't proven, the old sheriff would likely be back in the next election. Lewis understood that he could not win the battle with drugs and corruption alone. So, he did something extraordinary. Traditionally, there are few species more territorial than law enforcement: the sheriff's turf is his to rule, and rarely shared. But Lewis ignored that, got in his car, and drove an hour and a half to Savannah, the nearest Federal Bureau of Investigation (FBI) office, to beg for help.

As the FBI investigation progressed, they brought in the local federal prosecutors—a great trial lawyer and friend, Assistant US Attorney Fred Kramer. As it developed further, the US Attorney's Office thought that it was an appropriate case to use the RICO Act, so they asked for help from the US Department of Justice (DOJ) in Washington, DC, which is how a young Organized Crime and Racketeering Strike Force Trial Attorney, Dan Small, was told to get on a plane and see what the heck was going on down there.

The investigation proceeded. The Internal Revenue Service (IRS) was brought in to look at cash dealings. We were able to turn one of the deputies and convince him to wear a wire on the others, which resulted in some extraordinary tapes and further lines of investigation. Eventually, we drafted a RICO indictment and sent it up the line for approvals. But all that took time. To normal people in normal circumstances, the criminal process happens quickly or not all: crime, arrest, trial, jail. Simple. As the weeks and months passed, we got increasingly anxious calls from Sheriff Parker: the good people of Appling County were losing faith, afraid that so much time passing meant nothing would happen and the bad guys had won—just like they had told everyone they would.

At first, Lewis did little things to keep up appearances. For example, he put signs in front of his office that said, "FBI Parking," and had friends park their cars there. But as his calls got more desperate, more had to be done. So the FBI flew the US Attorney and me down to the county in their plane to reassure Lewis. Lewis then took us to lunch at a crowded local restaurant. The food was great, but I don't think Lewis ever sat down to eat: he spent the whole time going table to table greeting people. When I commented to one of the deputies, "he's quite the politician," he responded, "Oh no, not usually, he's just making sure that everyone knows you're with DOJ's Organized Crime and Racketeering Strike Force in Washington! As soon as they leave, that news will spread like wildfire. By tonight, the whole county will know you were here!"

Sure enough, by the time we got back to the sheriff's office, there was a phone message from an attorney whose office was across the street and who was a close associate of the former sheriff. He wanted to talk with the US Attorney. "He doesn't want to talk to some foreigner from DC," Lewis explained, "he thinks he can sweet talk the Georgia boy." But the US Attorney was having none of it, "You're coming with me, Dan," he said, "And you take the lead."

So, we left the sheriff and walked across the street. When the two of us walked in, Emmet (we'll call him) was surprised to see me, offered us both drinks (we declined), and started smooth talking about just wanting everyone to get to know each other and be on the same team. The US Attorney said simply, "Talk to him," pointing to me. I said, "Emmet, the party is over for you and your pals here in Appling County. The train is leaving the station, and you can either be on it or under it, I really don't give a damn. If you want to be on it, here's my card, call me. If you want to be under it, so be it. We're done here." And the US Attorney and I turned and walked out.

Back across the street, the sheriff and his deputies were anxiously awaiting a report of our meeting (which the US Attorney gave since I was still shaking with excitement) and loved it. That message might not travel as far as lunch had, but it would travel in the right direction.

The investigation continued to take time, and the sheriff's frustration grew. When he learned that there was a grand jury hearing evidence in Savannah, he insisted that he had to come talk to them. We tried to dissuade him: after all, he wasn't involved with the illegal activity so he really had no evidence to provide. But he insisted, and we were curious, so we gave in. The sheriff came to the grand jury and this big, tough sheriff broke down and wept: "You have to do something!" he pleaded, "You have to save my county! We're in terrible trouble, and you may be the only people who can help!" It was completely genuine; he cared so deeply about his home. By the time he was done, I felt like I should round up a bunch of horses for the grand jury so the posse could saddle up and ride out after the bad guys. Walking Tall.

Finally, we brought an indictment and teams of FBI agents down to the county before the first light one day to make coordinated arrests. Of course, the grand jury operates in secret, so I couldn't tell the sheriff anything about the indictment. I just told him that something was going to happen that day that might draw attention, so could he and his deputies provide security at the Appling County Courthouse? He continued pleading with me: "Mr. Small, I know you can't do everything, but if you could just get Larry . . .," or, "if you could just get Bob . . .". I knew that our indictment included everyone he named and more, but I could say nothing.

On the morning of the arrests, the sheriff pulled in every uniformed deputy he had to guard the courthouse, while he and his friend, the chief of police of Baxley, the county seat, waited anxiously inside. Out their window, to their amazement, they watched a parade of the county's royalty brought in handcuffs. Eighteen defendants in all. Finally, when we heard the last arrest had been made, we unsealed the indictment, I walked into the room where they were waiting, dropped a copy of the detailed, sixty-five-page, eighteen-defendant, indictment on the desk, and said "enjoy."

We lawyers get caught up with the law, the evidence, and the battle, and sometimes lose sight of the forest for the trees. In Appling County, the forest was a county at a tipping point and the people who cared deeply about it not knowing what to do. Of the many good memories of that case and its people, one of the best remains a simple one: The laughter and exclamations of joy coming out of that little room, as these two tough cops who cared saw things they had long suspected now written in black and white, people they had long suspected and even feared named as defendants, and their long-suffering hopes for the county they loved coming to life. There is no panacea, no perfect resolution, but that laughter and joy will always stay with me as a reminder that as trial lawyers, sometimes we can impact people's lives in surprising ways.

LAW AS A FORCE FOR CHANGE

The Racketeer Influenced and Corrupt Organization (RICO) law was passed in 1970, largely as a tool against the Italian Mafia. The idea was to address the mob's infiltration of legitimate businesses and provide a way to paint with a broad brush: not just focus on a single crime but show a pattern of racketeering activity, broadly defined. However, Congress cannot pass a law just for the Italian mob—too specific, or too discriminatory, depending on your point of view. So, the law makes no mention of the mob and is instead broadly and generically written. For the first years of its existence, defendants challenged the use of the law beyond the mob as being beyond Congress' intent. But the courts said no: the fight against the Mafia might have been the impetus for the law, but that's not what Congress wrote and passed.

The Department of Justice was concerned that the law's broad reach might tempt some prosecutors to abuse it, and the courts might react by striking down or limiting this important new tool. So, the DOJ required that all federal criminal RICO cases nationwide be reviewed and approved in Washington, DC. When I joined the Organized Crime and Racketeering Strike Force, reviewing proposed RICO cases became part of my job. Sometimes, as with Appling County, that included assisting in the investigation, development, and trial of RICO cases.

It was still early in the law's evolution and there were still hurdles along the way. The first hurdle was internal. After a great deal of work with the US Attorney's Office and the FBI, we drafted a proposed RICO indictment and supporting prosecution memo, and I brought it back to Washington, DC, with my recommendation that it be approved as soon as possible. But even though the law was broadly written, some still viewed it narrowly. The then Chief of DOJ's Criminal Division, Rudy Giuliani, would not approve the indictment. In his view, this wasn't what RICO was meant for.

Not to be deterred, the US Attorney and the Special Agent in Charge of the FBI in Savannah, Bill Hinshaw, borrowed an FBI plane and flew up to Washington, DC, to plead their case. They came to my office and we went to meet with Giuliani. He told us that RICO was not for redneck sheriffs in Georgia but for mobsters in New York. The US Attorney was furious, and responded that corrupt sheriffs were a very serious issue and that he wanted to be sure that he heard Giuliani correctly because he intended to take this up with the Attorney General. We left the meeting unhappily and with the issue unresolved. When we returned to my office to plot our next move, there was a message that the indictment had been approved up the line.

The second hurdle was in court. The judge—like most judges around the country at the time—had no prior experience with RICO, and he didn't like what he saw. Too broad, too vague. Individual crimes should be prosecuted individually, not as some "pattern." Reviewing a series of defense motions attacking the law and the indictment, he made clear his displeasure: cutting back some of the charges, narrowing and limiting our case for trial, and making clear that he might do more. We were hanging on by our fingernails, but we got to trial. Once there, we had strong evidence to present: in testimony, tape recordings, and exhibits—evidence of South Georgia law enforcement officers accepting bribes to protect drug smuggling. This might be old news in Miami, but it was new and profoundly shocking in rural South Georgia.

Slowly but surely, we could sense the judge's view of the case changing, sensed him getting angry. The tape recordings were clear and powerful. The level of corruption was deeply disturbing. The defense clung to the sympathetic ear they had pre-trial, but that ear had turned from sympathy to anger, and the defense wasn't listening. At the close of the government's case, they moved for a directed verdict. Denied. After the jury's guilty verdict, they moved to have it overturned. Denied. At sentencing, they presented the court with piles of letters of support, particularly for the former sheriff, Red Carter, who had ruled the county for 20 years. But the judge's shock at what he had heard was now clear. I don't have a transcript, but basically, the judge who had come so close to throwing our whole case out, now angrily declared:

"This will not happen in my Georgia!"

"Sheriff, I've read all these letters, but the letter writers did not hear the evidence. I did. And I don't have a good word to say about you, except that you're lucky the government didn't charge you with more, so I can't sentence you to more." Then gave him the maximum.

We did not decide to use this strange new law lightly. We knew it would present hurdles. But we also knew that we were dealing with a broad criminal enterprise that required us to be creative and aggressive if we were to present the judge and jury with a full picture. RICO gave us that opportunity. Being a trial lawyer requires you to try to make that match between the law and the facts in every case. Sometimes that's an easy process. Sometimes, like here, it requires persistence and determination. If you've thought it through carefully, and believe in your case, sometimes you can prevail.

"I LIED LIKE HELL!"

False testimony cuts to the heart of our system of justice. We depend on the witness's oath to tell "the truth, the whole truth, and nothing but the truth" to maintain the integrity of our system. When a witness lies at trial, it may keep vital evidence from the jury. But in some ways, perjury is even more damaging before the grand jury. At trial, the witness is subject to cross-examination, and if the jury decides they are lying, it can be devastating to their case, but the grand jury is responsible for sorting out what happened and who is responsible, who should be brought to trial and for what. Perjury interferes with both their investigative and screening functions.

And yet, people try it so often and believe they can get away with it. After all, they lie all the time and nothing happens. Nothing will happen here. What can this bunch of yahoos on a grand jury do that others cannot? Which is why prosecutions for perjury, though often difficult, are nevertheless so important. There has to be an answer to "nothing will happen."

Charlotte Lightsey was the wife of former Appling County Sheriff Joe Lightsey. She was also his deputy sheriff, and, according to several folks, both the brains and the brawn of that couple. As one of the players put it, "If you have to get caught in a dark alley with one of them, choose the sheriff: Charlotte is much more dangerous!" Everything we saw and heard supported that conclusion.

Once the investigation was well underway, we subpoenaed several of the corrupt law enforcement officers to the grand jury in Savannah to see what they would say. Some of them refused to answer, relying on their Fifth Amendment right against self-incrimination. Law enforcement officers, sworn to uphold the law, refusing to answer direct questions about taking bribes to protect drug smuggling because a truthful answer would incriminate them. An ugly scene, to be sure, but they were invoking their constitutional right.

Not Charlotte. She denied it all, vehemently and aggressively. She knew nothing about bribes, knew nothing about drug smuggling. She would never violate her oath of office as a deputy sheriff, and shame on those prosecutors for trying to bamboozle these good grand jurors with lies and rumors. It was quite a show.

The drive from the federal courthouse in Savannah down to Appling County at the time was about an hour and a half. Leaving the grand jury, Sheriff Lightsey was driving. Charlotte was in the passenger seat. Two of the sheriff's deputies were in the back seat. All four had grown up together in the county, known each other all their lives, and trusted each other completely. However, unknown to the other three, we had confronted one of the deputies, and he had eventually agreed to plead guilty and cooperate with the investigation. On this long drive home, he was wearing a wire, which picked up and recorded every word.

Naturally, the conversation turned to the grand jury. Many of the planeloads of drugs they protected were brought in on a Friday night, when everyone was at the other end of the county at the high school football game, and they named the loads by that week's opponent. So it was easy to ask about specific loads. Someone asked the sheriff what he said to the grand jury when we asked him about the "Reidsville load." "Oh, I took the Fifth on those questions," the sheriff replied, "I didn't want to answer questions about that. Who knows what they might know."

Charlotte was outraged at that show of weakness by her husband and boss. "What?" she said angrily, "you didn't just say no?" The sheriff was instantly defensive: "No, I didn't just say no, what did you say?" To which Charlotte responded, "Well I lied like hell! I did on a bunch of things!"

In the back seat, you could almost sense our cooperating deputy's unease. This was all fairly new to him. They were in a moving car. He didn't have an earpiece or anything. How sensitive was the tape recorder he was wearing? Did it really pick up the extraordinary thing Charlotte had just said? He didn't know that the machine had picked it up clear as a bell. So, just in case, you could hear him shuffle a bit, lean forward, and very innocently ask, "Do what, Charlotte?"

And Charlotte obliged. She turned around and explained to the deputy—right into the microphone—"I lied like a damn dog! They threaten you with perjury, they're not gonna charge anyone with any damn perjury, they're just saying that to try to scare you!" She was right, of course; we did say that to her and other witnesses to try to scare them into telling the truth. Too often, prosecutors don't have the evidence to back it up, and perjury helps obstruct an investigation. This time, we had good evidence, and that, combined with her taped admissions, was enough to indict her for perjury, among other crimes. We played that tape at her trial, and the jury convicted her. We played it again at her sentencing hearing, and an angry judge added the maximum five-year sentence for perjury on to her 15-year sentence for RICO and drug smuggling, for a total sentence of 20 years.

Charlotte Lightsey's sentence did not solve the problem of perjury before the grand jury by any means, but it highlighted some of the attitudes and assumptions that encourage it and the need for a strong response to protect our system of justice.

"JUST PRESS PLAY"

Testimony about conversations can be tough. If a witness testifies, "The defendant said X," the jury has a long road to travel before they get to "X": Is the witness telling the truth? Does the witness have reasons to lie? If they're not lying, are they mistaken? Did they hear it accurately? How long ago was it? Do they now remember it accurately? How was it said, what was the tone of voice? And so much more. All that before they even get to "X," and what it means. It's a lot.

But what if you could cut out all that interference and noise, and just hear the defendant *say* "X" directly in their own voice, their own tone, their own words? That's the power of tape recordings in a trial. The jury gets to hear it as it really happened, dramatically and undeniably. Done right, it can be overwhelming to the defense.

The government can obtain tape-recorded evidence in basically three ways, each with their own pros and cons. First is by a wiretap: a microphone planted in a particular place or a particular phone, generally by court order. This can be very productive, and many important cases have been brought as a result, but it can require a great deal of resources to monitor. And it can be very hit or miss: you have to have the bug in the right place at the right time, and wherever it is, you lose out if the targets go somewhere else or use another phone.

Second is by an undercover agent: someone who is trained and understands both what is needed to bring a case, and what the limits are on what they do or say to avoid entrapment or other problems. However, infiltrating a criminal organization with an undercover agent is difficult and risky, and even once inside, the undercover agent will often never get the same level of trust as long-time members of the group.

The third way is with a cooperator: someone who is part of the criminal activity but agrees to turn and cooperate with the government, including tape recording his former colleagues. Here, the trust of the others is presumably there, but the training is not. The cooperator is unlikely to know when he has said or done the wrong thing, when he has gone too far, or when he has created evidence that may help the defense.

In the Appling County case, we had the best of both worlds. When we confronted one of the corrupt deputy sheriffs, we were able to develop a witness who moved around freely with the targets, who was completely trusted since they'd grown up together, and who had enough law enforcement training to readily understand what we needed but also what the limits were. The results were extraordinary.

One of my favorites was a tape I mentioned earlier: When two of the deputies went to drug kingpin Larry Jackson's house to voice their concerns about the investigation, Jackson sought to reassure them by reminding them how much money they had made and would continue to make once the investigation blew over. But the conversation really got good when they got down to the numbers. Jackson had been giving the bribe money to the sheriff and relying on the sheriff to give the deputies their share.

Except he hadn't. "No honor among thieves." The sheriff had been giving the deputies less than he and Jackson had agreed, and pocketing the difference. When Jackson asked the deputies how much they had been paid for the different planeloads, and they told him, he was furious. "You've been f____ed," he said, "You've been f____ed bad!" Ahh, the power of tape. To help the deputies understand what a good guy he was, and how badly the sheriff had cheated them without his knowledge, Jackson called his wife, Suzette, who was also his bookkeeper, into the room, and angrily went through some of the loads with her: "I paid God-damn Sheriff Lightsey thirty God-damn thousand dollars for the Reidsville load, and he was supposed to pay each of you five God-damn thousand!" (I don't have the transcripts any more, so the numbers may be off, but you get the idea). And on it went, laying out the bribery payments in angry, excruciating detail, corroborated by the bookkeeper. All because the sheriff had cheated his friends. How does the defense argue against a tape like that?

They couldn't. We had, of course, provided the tapes and transcripts to defense counsel before trial. But tape cases were pretty rare in

Georgia at the time, and I'm not sure the defense counsel—even experienced as it was—fully understood the power of tapes—of its client's own voices filling the courtroom with open talk of drugs and bribes. In opening statements, several defense counselors attacked the government's case as groundless and promised the jury that when it came to their turn, their clients would take the witness stand and tell them what really happened.

It was a mistake. It was a promise they couldn't keep. By the end of the government's case, they understood the power of tapes, the impact on the jury, and the impossibility of contradicting what the jury had heard with their own ears. They realized that for each of them, if they took the stand, my cross-examination would feature "just press play," and they would have to relive the nightmare. Eleven defendants went to trial. In the end, only one of them (a minor player who had not been recorded—more on that later) took the stand. The rest had witnessed the power of tapes in court, and it sent them all to jail.

BRING OUT THE BAD STUFF

None of us are perfect, and so no witness is perfect. They all have issues in their backgrounds, in their involvement in the case, in their prior statements, and elsewhere. To prepare a witness, trial lawyers must:

1. develop some kind of bond to create enough trust for them to be willing to tell you the whole truth;
2. push the witness to get the full truth, good or bad;
3. work with the witness to figure out the best way to tell it—all of it—if need be.

What you don't know can hurt you. Badly. Tell your witness: whatever it is, we can deal with it. What we don't want is for the other side to bring it out because I didn't know about it. Then, it's not just the bad facts, it's the coverup. Something that could have been raised and dealt with on direct examination becomes powerful ammunition for cross. We used to say when I was a prosecutor: "**B**ring **O**ut the **B**ad **S**tuff!" or BOBS. Anything else just makes it worse.

In the Appling County case, BOBS was personified by Billy Breen. Billy was the broker, the middleman. If you're buying or selling a house, you might bring in a broker to help manage all the moving parts: buyer, seller, inspection, permits, financing, movers, whatever. The same is often true in complex criminal deals. That was Billy. He didn't *do* any of the physical crimes necessarily, but he brought everyone together: growers, importers, pilots, landing strip, loading crews, truckers, etc. That's what he did in Appling County, all the pieces of a criminal enterprise. And he was good at it.

Until, on an unrelated deal, after the Appling County deals, one or more of the parties thought Billy was cheating them. If you thought your real estate broker was cheating you, you might hire a lawyer to bring a lawsuit. Obviously, that resource is not available in the criminal world. Instead, one of the offended parties shot up Billy's house with an AK-47. Billy decided, after years on the criminal side of things, this was a sign that it was time to change sides. So he became a law enforcement informant, witness, and eventually an undercover operative. It all was pretty successful; he even wrote a book on his informant/undercover exploits.

Meanwhile, though, by pure happenstance, the trial of my Appling County case was the first time Billy would appear as a government witness. So, I was the first prosecutor to have to prepare him for testimony. The FBI had Billy stashed in a safe house in an old military facility outside of Savannah, so I went out there to spend a couple days preparing him for trial. From the beginning, it was clear that there was a problem.

Billy was smart, articulate, and proud. Too proud. He knew he was good at what he did and wanted everyone else to know it. He had been God's gift to the criminal world, masterminding complex deals around the country. Now, having changed sides, he was God's gift to law enforcement, using his considerable knowledge to promote justice. The bad guy had become a good guy. Except I knew that no one would buy it. The more Billy talked about what a blessing he was to law enforcement, the more I could imagine defense counsel using his life of crime to rip him apart. Juries don't believe in miraculous transformations, and they don't like phonies. Real change, and real redemption, takes much more. Billy's brand-new "good guy" posture, would be a disaster on cross.

I had to be diplomatic but firm. "Billy, I know how much help you will be to law enforcement, and the FBI knows, but defense counsel is going to bring out all the bad stuff. You have to be completely open and honest about bringing it out first." I went through this with him over and over, hour after hour, day after day, with limited success. Finally, on the second or third day, Billy looked at me sadly and said, "Dan, you want me to come across as a bad guy!" We were finally getting somewhere. "Bad but hoping to change," I said. "Question, Pause, Answer, Stop." Tell the whole truth.

After a lot more work, he did. Marvelously. Billy took the stand on direct and laid out his long history of crime. Openly, in great detail. If I missed some bad act along the way, he'd stop me and add it in. His testimony about the Appling County defendants fit right into that history. The jury was horrified at this life of crime but riveted. This was the real Billy, and it was clearly the truth. When I finally sat down, after two days on direct, we were all exhausted including defense counsel. Eleven defendants went to trial, and for a number of counsels—and clients—cross-examining this awful person was going to be a highlight. But Billy had preempted them. One after another, they got up to cross-examine, brought out some bad things they were going to beat Billy up with, but Billy could say, "Oh yeah, I talked about that on direct, do you want me to tell it again?" or "Yes, and there's something I forgot to mention, can I tell you that story, too?" They were lost. There was nowhere to go. Their clients were expecting a great show from counsel, but it was Billy who was grabbing the jury's attention. One by one they sat down, having gotten nowhere.

Finally, the last counsel got up on cross. We could see that he had a box of files, all carefully organized and marked, of bad things which to accuse Billy. But all he could do was look at his files forlornly. The jury had already heard it. Nevertheless, he tried nobly. He got up a head of steam, asked a bunch of aggressive questions about the bad stuff (which Billy agreed with), and finally, as a grand rhetorical flourish, he threw down his pen and shouted, "In fact, you haven't had an honest job in 20 years!" And sat down. Nice finish. Next witness. We all started shuffling our papers to move on.

But Billy hadn't been prepared to allow rhetorical questions. He had been prepared to tell the whole truth: "Question, Pause, Answer, Stop!" So, after a brief pause, when everyone thought he was done and they were focusing on what came next, he leaned forward into the microphone and said, "Actually, I think it's been 21 years since I had an honest job." And the jury, after all that tension, burst out laughing. Billy left the stand a career criminal, yet an honest man. Most witnesses' problems are not that dramatic, but whatever it is, develop trust, find out what it is, and Bring Out the Bad Stuff!

"A GOOD LICKIN'"

The wisdom of juries. I know, I know, it's popular to bash them. Yes, they are human and therefore capable of making mistakes (aren't lawyers human, too?). But I have also seen them show real wisdom. Sometimes we lawyers get caught up in our cases and lose sight of what's at stake. It can take a jury to remind us.

Larry Jackson's father, AZ, had grown up a dirt-poor farmer in Appling County and remained poor all his life until his son started making money in the drug business. Larry then used his father to help hide his illegal profits. Larry and his wife looked at a house to buy. They did all the looking, asked all the questions, talked about moving in, and did all the negotiations. But then at the closing they had scheduled, AZ was the only one who showed up, with a shopping bag full of cash, and bought the house in his own name.

They repeated this process with cars and other major purchases. Larry would find something he wanted, work out the terms of the purchase and everything else, but then AZ would show up with a bag of cash and buy it in his own name. We brought the IRS in, and they could find no real legitimate assets or income for AZ. But they scoured the county and found various other cash purchases. The house, though, was the biggest and most dramatic.

So, we indicted father and son on tax charges, in addition to the other charges against Larry. Did we care about AZ? Not too much: there was no direct evidence of his being involved in the drug business, though he clearly knew that the bags of cash didn't grow on pecan trees. The tax charges were a way of highlighting the laundering of cash and enlisting the IRS's help in doing so. Would we have dropped the charges against AZ for a deal with Larry? Probably. But we never had to make that choice. Larry insisted on going to trial, so AZ went to trial with him. Three Jacksons: father, son, and wife, now co-defendants.

It must have been tough for the father, sitting in court, listening to the tapes and other damning evidence against his only son and daughter-in-law. At the end of the government's case, there was little or nothing that Larry could do. He couldn't take the stand in the face of all the tapes. None of the defendants could, despite some of their lawyer's promises. Except AZ, against whom there were no tapes, just cash. Lots of it. Did he think the jury would believe him? Did he just feel that he had to do what he could to defend the family? Hard to say.

AZ Jackson took the stand and told a story that was, even in the telling on direct examination, with his own lawyer, ridiculous. He said that he knew nothing about the drugs. That he had done odd jobs over the years to make money, so that he could one day buy his son a house and other things. He kept the money under his mattress in his little shack. And so on. It was clearly nonsense. When it was over, I started to get up for cross-examination. My wise and wonderful partner at trial, Assistant US Attorney Fred Kramer, grabbed my sleeve and whispered, "Go easy on the old man. Who cares!"

So I did. At first. I was respectful and tried to ask gentle questions. But the story was so bad, he was so unprepared for cross, and he was such a bad liar that with each question, the story just got worse. I gradually got angry and started digging in. By the end of an hour or two of cross, through no great skill of mine, everyone understood that he was a liar and the story was nonsense. When I went back to our table, I somewhat sheepishly whispered to Fred, "Sorry." He smiled and said, "He deserved it."

The case was a complex one for the jury: Eleven defendants, a number of counts under several different statutes, and a variety of RICO legal issues raised by the defense. When the evidence closed and the jury went out to deliberate, we expected them to be out for some time. So, we were very worried when, after only about four hours, we got a call to come back to the courtroom: the jury had a question. This wasn't good: The jury must be hung up on some of the legal issues the defense had raised against count one, the RICO count.

When court reconvened, the judge asked the marshal to take the written question from the jury foreman and bring it up to the bench. The judge unfolded it, read it to himself, and then looked up at me, clearly trying to suppress a smile, and called all counsel up to the sidebar. "The jury's note reads as follows," he said, "On count seven, the tax charge, can we convict defendant Larry Jackson and let the old man go?" The judge looked up at me and asked, "Mr. Small?" Now it was my turn to try to suppress a smile.

The legal answer to the jury's question was easy: yes, of course, the jury could separate the defendants. But everyone at the sidebar realized the broader implications of the question. If the jury, after only four hours, was focused on count seven, that meant they had probably already dealt with counts one through six, and that was not a good omen for the defense. So, I responded to the judge, "Yes they can," all parties agreed, the judge gave the jury their answer, and within a couple more hours, the jury came back with its verdict: all defendants guilty on all counts, *except* AZ Jackson, not guilty on the tax charge.

In that district at that time, the lawyers could talk to the jurors after the verdict. It's a great opportunity for trial lawyers to learn, which too few courts allow. The jury had a number of helpful comments and insights, but the one that I remember best was on AZ Jackson. "Mr. Small," one of the jurors said, "we assume that our verdict will send the man's son and daughter-in-law to jail for a long time. We talked it over, and we agreed that what that old man needed was a good lickin', and you gave it to him, and that's probably enough."

Of course, they were right. Don't ever underestimate the collective wisdom of twelve people working hard to try to do the right thing. Respecting that effort emphasizes the challenge of presenting a case to them in ways they can understand and helping to guide them toward what's right. I don't know whether I went too far with my cross of AZ Jackson or just helped the jury reach the right result, or both. I tend to think it's both. But I was satisfied with the result, and it was a fun cross. Lessons learned.

3

U.S. v. Cammarata

EXECUTIVE SUMMARY

Drugs and multiple murder Racketeer Influenced and Corrupt Organizations Act (RICO) indictment of the "Godfather of Houston" and his gang.

As you read this chapter, be aware of:

- **Climbing the ladder**—Working up the chain of command, whether in a criminal gang or a legal corporation, is a common way of determining ultimate responsibility and is a common strategy, but not one without risks and obstacles.

- **"Bad Facts Make Bad Law"**—Sometimes, a legal principle gets too caught up in its own technicalities and needs to be challenged on its merits.

- **Juror #6**—Do not underestimate the wisdom of jurors or their desire to do the right thing. But at the same time, do not underestimate the challenges they face. Present your case in ways that help them to understand and to do the right thing.

U.S. v. CAMMARATA

Sam Cammarata was from Boston originally. The rumor was that he had been a cop at some point, but I don't know if we ever confirmed that. He had ties to the tightly organized Boston Mafia, but not strong enough to advance him as fast as he wanted. So, he set off in search of fame and fortune in the criminal world. He spent some time in Louisiana, working for New Orleans Godfather Carlos Marcello, but that tight-knit organization was also hard to move up in from the outside.

Sam moved on and ended up in Houston, which turned out to be the city of his dreams. Here was a booming metropolis without any real pre-existing organized crime structure. Sam set out to become the Godfather of Houston. He came pretty close. Sam recruited various other criminals to join his organization, most notably Tommy Teustch, a cunning but very violent criminal. Tommy always carried two guns and bragged about using them. His love of the good life, money, and killing set the tone for the Cammarata organization.

THE CRIMINAL NEXT DOOR

Early on, Sam took over a nightclub, which provided him three key things. First, it was a good cover: Sam's family and neighbors believed—or maybe they wanted to believe—that Sam was a legitimate business owner and music promoter. Second, it provided a base of operations where people could easily come and go, meet, and plan. Third, it was an easy way to launder the illegal profits: who knows whether a cash bar sells $100 of drinks in an evening or $1,100, and who knows how many people actually pay for admission with cash.

From the nightclub, Sam built an empire of traditional criminal activity: bookmaking, loansharking, prostitution, extortion, and more. All of this, thanks to Tommy's involvement, with a particularly violent aspect. The organization, and its profits, grew. Sam was on his way to achieving his goal: Godfather of Houston. All this behind a front of legitimacy.

Sam did spend time managing the nightclub and various musical acts. And he encouraged other members of his organization to be involved in legitimate businesses and community activities: church, school, social, whatever. Tommy, his right-hand man, bought a bowling alley. What a strange disconnect: a professional criminal and killer, entertaining families and working people with bowling. It happened to be another good way to launder illegal cash (bowling shoes, anyone?), but it was a real business.

It worked—to some extent. The veneer of legitimacy kept law enforcement's attention away from them for a time. Even when things came crashing down, it still helped. Fast forward to when we indicted the organization, we charged thirteen people with racketeering and other crimes. The Texas Rangers and other cooperating agencies coordinated sending arrest teams across Texas to arrest all of the defendants quickly, before news of the indictment got out. However, there were only a few of us prosecutors, and we spent the day of the arrests racing from one courthouse to another to attend bail hearings to keep them in jail.

But Tommy was prepared. There had been rumors of an investigation, so he had a package ready. As I was racing across the state trying to get in front of the local magistrate holding his bail hearing, Tommy's lawyer got there first and argued that Tommy was not a danger or a flight risk: he had deep roots in the community, was a church Deacon, had family, and had the deed to his bowling alley ready to put up as security. The local magistrate was convinced and let him go before I could get there to argue the other side.

In an instant, Tommy was gone, off to Costa Rica. He stayed based there for several years, but his love of the high life—the clubs, the women, the parties—was so strong that he kept coming back to Texas for a few days at a time. Still, he remained a step ahead. Although we were in federal court, in part to make use of the federal RICO Act, the case was largely investigated by the Texas Rangers. The Rangers put out a substantial reward for information leading to his capture and pressured their informants. But their informants' fear of Tommy outweighed the temptation of the reward, so we'd get calls like:

"Tommy was here!"

"When?"

"Yesterday!"

"Where is he now?"

"Don't know!"

"Why didn't you call yesterday?"

"Um, couldn't get to a phone!"

The Rangers would call in a Special Weapons and Tactics (SWAT) team since Tommy was always heavily armed and had sworn never to be taken alive, to see if he was still where the informant claimed to have seen him. Of course, he never was. Back to Costa Rica.

Tommy being on the loose, combined with his vow to never be taken alive and to exact vengeance on his enemies, led the Rangers to instruct me to always travel with them in a group and always carry a gun when I was in Texas. We finally got word six years later that this "pillar of the community" died in Mexico, where he had gone for back surgery.

The veneer of legitimacy went beyond business. It included family. Sam kept to the traditional Mafia practice of keeping family and business separate. His family went with him to church and community events, and heard only about Sam and his friends' legitimate business activities. Sam's mother, an immigrant from Italy, who spoke limited English, lived with them. She was a great cook, and every Sunday, Mama Cammarata would put together a feast for Sam and his friends. Sam would invite all kinds of people, including members of his organization, but the ironclad rule was: no talk of business at the table. So seasoned criminals and cold-blooded killers sat around the Sunday dinner table with everyone else, enjoying homemade pasta, homemade meatballs, and good Italian wine.

Sam's indictment on racketeering and murder charges was a shock to many people, including his family: it wasn't fair, it was all lies, he was being persecuted. That's what he told them, and that's what they believed. When the trial started, his wife was there, sitting right behind him in the front row. Sam's lawyer in his opening statement made a show of pointing her out and talking about her support. She would be there for the whole trial, he promised. But our beliefs, even those we hold so dear, are rarely confronted with a tidal wave of sworn testimony and other evidence. Hour after hour, day after day, his wife had to listen to compelling evidence that the husband she thought was a legitimate businessman, a gracious host, and a family man was, in fact, the head of a violent criminal organization. By the fourth day of this month-long trial, she was gone, never to return to the courtroom to support the "criminal next door."

CLEAN CRIME, DIRTY CRIME

The Cammarata organization engaged in a wide range of traditional criminal enterprises: Loansharking, prostitution, bookmaking, theft, extortion, you name it. But not drug dealing. Despite all those ugly crimes, in the traditional Mafia world that Sam Cammarata came from, drugs were "dirty." Only punks or druggies sold drugs. And drugs could hurt families, even Mafia families. Kill if you had to, but don't sell drugs. Sounds strange, but it was a real distinction for some time.

Ahh, but as the Bible says, "the love of money is the root of all evil."[1] And selling drugs, it turns out, makes money. *Lots* of money. Sam and his associates watched while no-good young punks made more money on one drug deal than they might make in a month of their crimes. And so, finally, they got into the drug business. They made money, but not as much as they'd hoped, held back in part by two problems: they were overly ambitious and overly violent.

The ambition problem was highlighted in Lebanon, of all places. One member of the organization, it turned out, had some Lebanese contacts. After some back and forth, they began discussion of an extraordinary guns-for-drugs deal with people in Lebanon. But Cammarata's people oversold their access to the high-end weapons the Lebanese wanted. And when they sent someone to negotiate the drug part of the deal, it got worse. A young hood who had basically never been out of Texas, walking the streets of Beirut, trying to negotiate with Lebanese drug lords. He was lucky to get out alive, and the deal never happened.

The other problem was violence. Tommy believed that violence was the answer to most everything. So that's how they approached the drug business. They would set up a drug buy, and then assault or murder the sellers and steal their drugs. Or they would set up a drug sale, and then assault or murder the buyers and steal their money. It made for quick and easy profits. But then they couldn't figure out why they weren't making as much money over time as the punk dealers.

Their confusion on this seems strange, but it was real. Any good businessman could have told them: true success in a business like this is not defined by the first sale. It's defined by developing relationships, repeat business, and secure transactions. It didn't take long for the word to get out within the drug community: "Stay away from these guys, they'll rip you off!" They made money but not the riches they had dreamed of that had lured them into the business in the first place.

I WAS JUST PLAYING A ROLE

To effectively investigate and prosecute many types of crimes, including organized crime, law enforcement needs to find a way inside the organization. So they rely, in part, on informants: people who are part

---

[1] Timothy 6:10 KJV.

of or close to the criminal activity but, for various reasons, are willing to provide information. It makes sense: these are crimes that are planned, and often committed, in secret. It would be foolish to think law enforcement should just wait and hope that they might stumble upon criminal activity. That's not the way the world works. They need to be pointed in the right direction. They need to get inside information.

Alas, the criminals know that. They know law enforcement needs them. The result is a difficult, sometimes dangerous, balancing act, with both sides asking, "what's in it for me?" and "what's the other guy doing?" Since the informant game is generally played in secret—like the criminal game—it can be subject to deception, mistakes, and abuse on both sides. A necessary evil is still an evil and has to be handled with great care.

To succeed in his work, Sam Cammarata actually had three roles to play. One was in his position as head of a criminal organization. The second, we've discussed, was his cover as a legitimate businessman and family man. But the third was as a secret informant, and Sam milked that role for all it was worth. To the question, "what's in it for me?" Sam's answer was, "a lot!" In three acts.

Act One started years before when Sam was caught carrying drugs. He was able to negotiate a deal with the Drug Enforcement Administration (DEA) to "work off" his bust by informing on other drug dealers and criminals of various sorts. He did that for several years until the DEA realized that he was playing them: among other things, he was informing on rivals, and then stepping in and taking over their business when they got busted. The DEA was unwittingly helping to expand the Cammarata criminal organization. So they cut him off as an informant. But Sam had discovered that there were benefits to being an informant—if you played it right.

For Act Two, Sam became an informant for the Central Intelligence Agency (CIA). He touted his international contacts to convince them that he could provide useful information. Of course, he didn't bother to tell them that he had abused his informant role with the DEA and they had kicked him out as a result. Nor did he tell the DEA that he had just changed agencies. It being the CIA, everything is secretive, so we never really found out all that Sam had told them or what he got in return. But the relationship supposedly continued right up until Sam was indicted, which led to the next Act.

Act Three was the trial. It's not uncommon in criminal cases for the government to try to "work its way up to the ladder," to convince underlings in criminal activity to testify against the next rung up the ladder, and so on. After all, the government should put particular focus on those at the top, and that's an important and often necessary way to get there. However, you have to give something to get something, and that can create issues for the testimony of those pointing up the ladder.

It's not uncommon for those at the top of the ladder to have insulated themselves from responsibility and then try to use that insulation to attack those trying to point the finger up, claiming things like:

- They're dishonest criminals;
- They did these crimes, not me;
- The government bought their testimony;
- Where's the evidence I ordered them to do this, other than from them?

If there isn't other evidence corroborating the finger pointer—tapes, emails, other witnesses—it can be a tough sell to a jury.

Sam took this defense, and then used his work as an informant to add another layer: "I wasn't really a criminal mastermind, I was just playing a role, so I could gather information for the government as an informant. Now, these criminals who actually did the crimes (drugs, murder, etc.) are just pointing the finger at me to get a better deal." After all, no one testified that Sam killed anyone or sold any drugs. They just claimed that he ordered them (nothing in writing, of course) to do it. And he was, indeed, an informant.

At trial, we had to come at it from two principal angles. First, spending time with our cooperating witnesses to emphasize Sam's integral and leadership role in the organization. Second, making clear (to the extent we could, given the secrecy) that he never told the DEA or the CIA about the murders and much else, and they did not and would not authorize him to be involved in such crimes. But it gave the defense something they are often missing: a motive and explanation for his actions. Not an easy fight.

In the end, after a long hard month of trial, we had developed a great deal of evidence on both of those themes. In closing argument, I was able to compare the "playing a role" defense to an octopus, "which, when cornered, exudes a cloud of black ink, and tries to slither away. The evidence here allows you, the jury, to see through the defendant's cloud of black ink. Don't let the defendant slither away." They didn't. Guilty on all charges. Sentence: forty-five years. Sam died in jail some years later.

ACTORS ON A STAGE

"All the world's a stage,
And all the men and women merely players;
They have their exits and their entrances,
And one man in his time plays many parts . . ."

–Shakespeare, *As You Like It*

All trial lawyers are frustrated actors on some level. Our stage is the courtroom, our stories are our cases, our script is the strange language of question and answer, and our audience is, of course, the jury. But one way to infiltrate a secret criminal organization is using an undercover agent, and when we try cases involving undercover agents, we realize that our performance is so much more controlled, easier, and safer.

We teach trial lawyers to "be yourself," don't try to be someone else. But an undercover agent has to create a persona that is a strange combination of himself/herself and someone else. Then they have to use that persona to win the trust of suspicious and dangerous strangers. Extraordinary. The best agents can do it without anyone even realizing it's happening. In the investigation into the Cammarata organization, I had the privilege of working with the best I've ever seen.

Benny, as we'll call him, was a Texas Ranger, an experienced investigator, and an undercover agent. He grew up on a ranch in West Texas, and his cover was usually as a wealthy West Texas rancher so he could talk about cattle, well, "until the cows come home." He was bright and personable, but it was more than that. He had a magnetic personality. If you walked into a bar full of strangers with Benny, somehow, within an hour or so, half the bar were your friends. And you couldn't tell how it happened, but you know that it doesn't happen when you walk into a bar *without* Benny.

True story. One night before the trial in Austin, I was working late preparing, so I agreed to swing by a local bar whenever I was done and meet a group of the Rangers from the case team for drinks, including

Benny. Apparently, before I arrived at the bar, they had befriended two guys who set off the Rangers' collective "Spidey Sense": something didn't seem right about these two: drug dealers? They needed to know more. So, without any of the Rangers mentioning what they did for a living, they sat with these two for several hours, drinking, playing liar's poker, and gently probing.

Then, after a couple hours, I walked into the bar, and I don't look or sound like a West Texas rancher. But Benny understood the problem and had anticipated it. He had already set the stage: mentioned to the two guys that he was doing a land deal and waiting to meet with his lawyer who (for some good reason I can't remember) had come down from up North, to help put the deal together. Fair enough, except that I knew nothing about this invented story. After a long day preparing for trial, I was just looking for a drink.

But Benny understood that, too. So, when I came into the bar and walked over, Benny grabbed my arm, just a little too hard, and pulled me down into a chair, saying, "Dan, how's that land deal coming? You know I forgot to mention . . ." and on he went with some story he'd invented about the invented land deal, just to give me time to understand and adjust. All part of the show. So, I joined in for a couple more hours of drinking, probing, and liar's poker. Eventually, the Rangers' unspoken collective wisdom decided that these two guys were actually OK, and imagine their surprise when someone casually let it drop that the fellows they'd been hanging out with all evening were all Texas Rangers—except for that one lawyer from up North.

Another true story. Throughout the pre-trial and month-long trial, we had a team of eight to twelve Rangers gathered in Austin from all around the state. They were great guys, professional and indefatigable. But they also loved to party. With input from the local Rangers, they developed a schedule of the big warehouse-style country-western dance halls outside of Austin. Monday was Free Drink Night at one place, Tuesday was Ladies Night at another, etc. And no matter how hard I worked them, they would want to go out drinking and dancing every night and invited me along.

I couldn't do it. I explained that I was working too hard to get ready for trial (and then in trial) and needed all my energy for that. At this stage of the case, they were mostly spending time waiting for me to need something. The compromise we worked out was Wednesdays:

Nickel Beer Night at the Silver Dollar, where we would be until closing time every Wednesday. But I discovered a cultural difference: as
Texans, they would meet someone and spend the night drinking, dancing, and talking, without anyone mentioning what they did for work. It
just wasn't important. But I was from the Northeast, where "So, what
do you do for work?" is usually one of the first questions when you
meet someone. The Rangers realized—correctly—that at a country-
western honky-tonk in Texas, "I'm a prosecutor with the Organized
Crime and Racketeering Strike Force of the U.S. Department of Justice
in Washington" just wasn't going to work.

So one night, sitting around a bar, I learned how it was done.
I learned from this group of experts all about developing an undercover persona. Not for any nefarious purpose, just to get me through
Wednesday nights without strange looks and rejection. Relentlessly, they
asked me about myself: my background, jobs I had held (there had been
many), family, etc. They explained that a good undercover persona was
not a complete invention. It should be based, as much as possible, on
real life, real experiences. I had to appear comfortable with it, able to
talk about it, tell jokes and stories, but without being self-conscious or
nervous. To be as natural as possible, it had to be as real as possible,
and yet not something so special that someone might follow up on it or
pursue it too far.

Finally, after much discussion and some debate, they came to an
agreement. One of my summer jobs in college had been as a mailman
for the US Post Office. That would work. It was interesting, occasionally
funny, but not threatening or intimidating. And they could make it fit.
I was a mailman from up North, in town for a mailman convention (they
assured me that there are conventions for everything). They talked me
through all the details in case they ever came up, and peppered me with
questions to see how I responded.

And it worked, sort of. I used my new "cover" a couple of times
at the Silver Dollar, and it was certainly more sociable than the whole
DOJ thing. But far more valuable to me was the hands-on lesson
on the methods and challenges of undercover work from a team of
experts.

Infiltrating the Cammarata organization took those same skills but
with so much more at risk. Despite the danger, Benny was able to get an
introduction to one of the members and then slowly, patiently, work his

way in. A big milestone was when he was invited to one of Mama Cammarata's Sunday dinners at Sam's house: endless delicious homemade Italian food, lively conversation, and a room full of criminals and murderers. Slowly, Benny became accepted as one of them.

Ultimately, Benny was able to gather important information about the organization's activities and was a key witness at trial. Meanwhile, once the investigation and his role came out, the relationships he'd developed with several of the members of the group still allowed him to help us persuade them to turn, plead guilty, and provide key testimony for the government. So undercover work played several key roles in the case. Actors on a stage.

BAD FACTS MAKE BAD LAW

When law enforcement breaks the law, they should not reap the benefits of their unlawful conduct. That's the theory behind the exclusionary rule: when law enforcement obtains evidence by some illegal means, that evidence should be excluded from use at trial. The hope is to both avoid an injustice against the defendant and to deter law enforcement from future illegality. But, of course, excluding evidence means that you are depriving the jury, the finder of fact, of important facts, and that may allow a criminal to go free. So how far do we go down that road? Bad cases had made bad law.

Unlike in legitimate business, when criminals meet, they don't often introduce themselves formally, and exchange contact information ("Here's my card!"). As a result, one well-established member of the Cammarata organization we knew only as "Dennis," so in the indictment, we charged Dennis LNU (Last Name Unknown) and gave a description. An arrest warrant was issued on that basis. As the Rangers arrested and questioned other members of the organization, they learned more about Dennis, including his name and address.

With that information and believing that they had to move quickly before Dennis learned of the indictment and fled, they went to the address. Dennis's roommate opened the door and stepped back, the Rangers walked in, and there was Dennis on the couch. They arrested him and took him in. Dennis apparently decided that the party was over, and almost immediately started confessing. Within hours, he had dictated and signed a detailed and chilling eight-page confession to, among other crimes, execution-style, cold-blooded murders. We expected him to plead guilty and cooperate against Cammarata.

But then Dennis got another lawyer who saw that the arrest warrant had no last name, and discovered a disputed line of cases that basically said that the Rangers should have gone back to the court and obtained a new, more complete warrant with the new information they had obtained. The defense filed a motion to suppress the confession, and we were shocked when the judge agreed. He found that the Rangers acted in good faith and reasonably believed that the arrest warrant was proper, but technically it was not. Since the confession followed from the technically deficient arrest, under the exclusionary rule as it then stood, the entire confession had to be excluded.

We were angry and decided to appeal. Several cases at the time had begun to explore the idea of a "good faith exception" to the exclusionary rule. If law enforcement acted reasonably and in good faith, did it really make sense to exclude otherwise admissible evidence? To what end? Our case, we thought, was as strong as you could get to support that idea, a voluntary confession to cold-blooded murder excluded based on a disputed technical issue that the arresting officers knew nothing about.

We appealed the judge's decision to suppress to the Fifth Circuit U.S. Court of Appeals. We argued that we understood the purpose of the exclusionary rule, to deter unlawful conduct, but that purpose didn't apply here, and the damage to justice was too great to apply the rule arbitrarily. Amazingly, the Court of Appeals agreed. In a powerfully worded opinion, the court reversed the judge's suppression order. After a careful analysis of the law and the arresting officers' actions, the Court held:

> "We question on these facts the claimed teaching value of the **exclusionary rule**. Suppression would teach, but the lesson would be one of cynicism and disrespect for a rule of law so wooden as to require application even when its purpose is not served. . . . In short, the marginal increment in deterrence that could be achieved by applying the **exclusionary rule** does not justify the societal costs of denying the jury access to Mahoney's confession."[2]

---

[2] U.S. v. Mahoney, 712 F.2d 956, 962 (5th Cir. 1983).

The defense filed for the case to be heard in the Supreme Court, and we prayed that the court would take the case. The good faith exception was still relatively new and unsettled law, and we thought that our case was a good one to settle it. Alas, the Supreme Court declined to hear the case, which was a win for us, leaving the Court of Appeals decision in place, but a disappointment in that sense. Ultimately, the court took another case and adopted the good faith exception as the law of the land. Bad facts no longer made bad law in a good case.

LADIES AND GENTLEMEN OF THE JURY

A trial lawyer's relationship with the jury is a strange one. In what other situation are you together in a room with people for long hours, dealing with difficult issues, but unable to talk? The jurors are trying to solve a puzzle, using information you give them, but they can't ask you questions or ask you to explain or repeat something. You are trying to persuade the jury your position is right, but you can't speak to them individually or hear their concerns. It's a strange and challenging situation trying to develop a relationship without the most important tools: listening and talking together.

Yet it happens. If you work at it consistently, and you're lucky, you develop a bond with the jury. The Cammarata case must have been a tough one for a jury:

- Disturbing, graphic testimony about cold-blooded murders;
- Confusing testimony about strange dealings in Lebanon;
- Bad guys turned government witnesses and good guys turned undercover agents;
- And through it all, Sam's "I was just playing a role" informant defense.

During the month-long trial, the jury worked hard. Nine to five was a short trial day for the judge, and the case was complex and contentious. And yet, slowly but surely, we bonded. It came out in small ways, in looks, gestures, and small incidents. Here are two small examples.

The judge did not give long lunch breaks. After all, the marshals brought in lunch for the jury, so they were ready to go fairly soon. So, each day, we would hurry down the street to a restaurant for a quick bite.

One day, we took a lunch break in the middle of my direct examination of an important witness. Running late leaving the restaurant, I caught my finger badly in the closing door. The guard at the courthouse had what looked like an old army surplus first aid kit (not sure which war). It was the only thing available, so we hurriedly wrapped my finger in old, yellowed gauze and went back to work.

There I stood all afternoon, questioning a witness, while holding my throbbing, badly wrapped finger. Finally, the court called the mid-afternoon break, and I could try to re-wrap it while someone found me some aspirin—in the middle of which the lead jury marshal came out of the jury room, over to my table, leaned over with a smile, and whispered, "Jury wants to know what you did to your finger?" I told him about being late leaving the restaurant and foolishly catching it in the door.

Court reconvened, the jury filed back in, and one after another of them gestured toward my finger (or theirs) and smiled at my mishap. The pain of the finger continued through the day, but it was far outweighed in my mind by the pleasure of having made that small connection. The Rangers finally brought me to the Emergency Room that night, still holding my throbbing finger. When I told the doctor that it happened at lunchtime, he said, "What the heck have you been doing that you didn't come in hours ago?" I smiled and said, "Connecting."

The courtroom for the Cammarata trial was fairly narrow, which led to a somewhat odd arrangement: both counsel tables were near the jury box, with the government's table in front of the defense table, which led to one of the other connection incidents. At one of the breaks, when I was out in the hall, the jury marshal came up to me and quietly said, "Just thought you'd like to know that defense counsel is trying to read your notes from behind you; Jury told me."

I was shocked it was happening, but again pleased that the jury cared. I didn't say anything to the defense counsel, but when court reconvened, I took out a fresh pad and wrote in large letters, "HI BOB!" (not his real name). Sure enough, at the next break, he came up to me quite upset, and insisted "I wasn't reading over your shoulder!" Since I hadn't specifically said that he was, I took that as both a confession and assurance that he wouldn't try it again.

But oftentimes you can't make an apparent connection or read what a juror is thinking. You just have to have faith. It's popular to bash juries, not have faith in them. Do they make mistakes? Of course they do; they're human. But I do have faith in their collective wisdom and how hard they try to get it right. The extreme example of all this from the Cammarata trial was Juror #6.

Juror #6 was a Hispanic fellow, high school education, regular job, no apparent reason to exclude him from the jury. So, there he sat in the front row. From the first day, he just sat there, staring off into space. I could not get him to look at me or the witness. I was angry: I was trying a very difficult month-long trial and I needed a unanimous jury for a conviction. If Juror #6 has checked out, the whole trial becomes a roll of the dice: which way did he decide, if at all, before he checked out?

I tried every trick I could think of to get his attention: dropping my pen right in front of him so I could get close, trying to hand him the documents that were being passed to the jury, but nothing worked. The rest of the jury was angry with him, too. In such an intense trial, the jury became very close, but during breaks, Juror #6 would just sit silently in the corner. We talked about asking the judge to kick him off the jury, but there didn't seem to be enough of a basis: he wasn't sleeping, he just appeared to be focused elsewhere. So he stayed.

At the close of the evidence, when the jury went back to start their deliberations, we were all in for a surprise. The first time someone couldn't remember a piece of evidence, Juror #6 provided it. And the next fact, and the next one. Couldn't remember the judge's instruction on a particular point? Juror #6 had it. And so on. He very quickly went from a concern to the jury to their hero. Why? It turns out that Juror #6 had never been asked to sit in a chair and just listen eight hours a day (none of us has). But to him, this was the most important thing he had ever done. How was he supposed to fulfill this important duty? The best solution he could come up with was to tune out everything else, ignore all distractions, and just listen. If that meant staring off into space, so be it. That's what he did, and for him it worked.

I think about Juror #6 often. I often talk about him when I'm teaching lawyers and witnesses. As trial lawyers, we are storytellers, teachers, and advocates. But we have to do all those things without feedback from the real audience. So we have to assume that they are listening and want to understand, and for us to take the responsibility of telling our story, teaching our lesson, and advocating our case in ways that are accessible and meaningful to Juror #6. He's trying hard to listen: give him a chance, give him a reason, give him something worth listening to. Therein lies the real challenge of trying cases.

4

Bert Lance

EXECUTIVE SUMMARY

Prosecution of former U.S. Budget Director in Atlanta for bank fraud.

As you read this chapter, be aware of:

- **Home cooking**. Understand the importance of developing and monitoring your relationships and reputation.

- **"Question, Pause, Answer, Stop!"** Being a witness is a scary and unnatural event. Succeeding in that difficult environment requires hard work and extensive preparation.

- **"When everything is important, nothing is important."** Resist the natural temptation to overload your case with detail. Cut it down as much as possible to a simple story that the jury can relate to and understand.

BERT LANCE

Bert Lance was a man of many facets. He was a Georgia banker (a "country banker," he called himself) who became embroiled with the scandal plagued, Pakistani-based Bank of Credit and Commerce International (BCCI). He was jovial, clever, and credited with popularizing the phrase,

"If it ain't broke, don't fix it." He was a politician who became a close friend and advisor to Jimmy Carter. When Carter was elected President, with Lance's help, Carter rewarded him by appointing him the powerful Director of the Office of Management and Budget (OMB).

Lance's appointment to OMB was not without controversy. Fellow Democrat Sen. William Proxmire (D-Wisc.) said, "He has none—zero, zip, zilch, not one year, not one week, not one day" of experience in managing something of the magnitude of the federal budget. But with a new incoming President, the nomination sailed through. Lance became one of the most powerful members of the "Georgia Mafia" that came in with President Carter, based on both their personal and professional relationships. He was dubbed the "Assistant President" by *Forbes* magazine and supposedly prayed together with the President every morning.

But Lance was touched by scandal before, during, and after his time in Washington. According to the *Washington Post*, "Lance was investigated by no fewer than eight different federal agencies . . . but he was never convicted of a crime and never went to jail." Some of the scandals got close enough, that Lance resigned from OMB under pressure in 1977, less than nine months after assuming office. In May 1979, the U.S. Department of Justice (DOJ) obtained a grand jury indictment in Atlanta against Lance and three associates, charging them with violating U.S. banking laws in a conspiracy to illegally obtain millions of dollars in loans. As the case headed to trial in the fall, as a brand-new lawyer just weeks into my job at DOJ, I wangled an assignment as the low man (#4 or 5, as I recall) on the totem pole of the trial team. My initial role was to do research and writing on our pretrial and trial motions and other pleadings. Just to be on the team was exciting.

LEARN FROM THE MASTERS

Part of the excitement of being on the team was learning from great lawyers—on both sides. The DOJ team was led by Ed Tomko and Marvin Loewy. Eddie was with DOJ's Fraud Section at the time, and was a funny, irreverent, and very talented trial lawyer. He loved trials and the process of putting a case together, and I learned a lot about the substance and the joy of trial work.

Marvin was on loan to the case from his position as deputy chief of DOJ's Organized Crime and Racketeering Strike Force. Also a talented trial lawyer, he was a great tactician, and I learned a lot about trial strategy. He also had a great sense of humor and an inscrutable poker face. One small example: several of our team were going out to a restaurant for dinner one night. As we approached the hostess station, Marvin made his way to the front of the group, looked the hostess straight in the eyes, and said: "Bond, James Bond, party of six."

The hostess was frozen in place: What to do? Surely, this was a joke, and she should laugh at it. But just as surely, there must be real people out there with that name (the internet says there are more than 1,000 in the United States), and no hostess wants to insult a guest by laughing at their name. She searched Marvin's poker face for some sign of humor but in vain. Finally, after a long pause, she pulled herself together, and bravely said, "Yes, Mr. Bond, right this way!" The rest of us barely kept it together until we were alone at the table, then laughed heartily.

Lance's lead defense lawyer was a distinguished Southern gentleman and highly regarded Atlanta trial lawyer. He was organized and smooth in his arguments to the court, and I learned a lot watching him. As the case progressed, I was allowed to argue some of the motions—a great opportunity just months out of law school. One of the things that impressed me in the motion hearings was how easily the lead defense counsel bonded with the magistrate or judge. How could I learn to do that?

Then, in one of the hearings, I learned that that bond was the result of a mix of ingredients: skill and experience, yes, but also a large dollop of home cooking. We had been arguing motions to the magistrate (I have no memory of the issues, as I recall there were a number of hearings), acting as the dignified counsel for our respective parties. Then the magistrate ordered a brief break. At which point, defense counsel sauntered up to the bench and, within my hearing, said, "So, Paul (or whatever the magistrate's name was), you coming duck hunting with us again this weekend?" There was some further laughing exchange I couldn't hear, then counsel sauntered back to his table. On the way past my table, he winked at me.

"With us?" "Again?" "This weekend?" Months out of law school, I was still imbued with the rules against *ex parte* contact between litigants and the judge. What was going on here? Home cooking. The easy bond that counsel had with the judges came from years of local efforts—in court and out of court, professional and social. I suppose I could have objected to duck hunting, but would that have improved my client's chances in court? Probably not. Better to learn from the masters that developing and monitoring your relationships and reputation can be almost as important as developing and maintaining your legal skills.

THE IMPORTANCE OF WITNESS PREPARATION

There is nothing natural about a courtroom. The layout, the people, how we act, how we communicate: all of this and more is dramatically different from the real world, from a natural conversation. Even the rhythm of question and answer is unnatural. "Question, Pause, Answer, Stop." How can lawyers expect normal people to deal with such an unnatural environment without a lot of help? We cannot. We must not. Preparing witnesses is one of the most important parts of trial work, yet too often it is shortchanged or ignored entirely.

In a well-tried case on both sides, Lance's team made a tactical error. They presented the court with a long list of character witnesses they were going to call in Lance's defense. Too long. As I remember, there were fifty-three of them, but who knows. Too many. And rather than impressing the judge, it upset him.

Character testimony has faded somewhat from the trial scene. But under FRE 405, it is most commonly, ". . . evidence of a person's character . . . proved by testimony about the person's reputation . . ."[1] It's basically people who know nothing about the facts of the case testifying that, "The defendant is a good guy, he would not have done these terrible things!" Okay, as far as it goes, but fifty-three of them? Too far.

The judge, undoubtedly with the visions of days or even weeks of this largely irrelevant testimony dancing in his head, exercised his prerogatives as a federal judge to drastically limit the questioning. Without diving into the murky law of character testimony, they were essentially limited to four legalistic questions about reputation. Incompressible to ordinary mortals.

The defense went ahead. They didn't call fifty-three character witnesses, but they did call a few. The most notable was Miss Lillian. Miss Lillian was the elderly and, I should say, saintly mother of the sitting President of the United States Jimmy Carter. She was called in her home

---

[1] Fed. R. Evid. 405(a).

state of Georgia to testify for the local "country banker" whom both she and her son knew well.

Preparing Miss Lillian for her testimony would have been easy, wouldn't it? "Miss Lillian, look here: the judge has limited us to these four legalese questions. I don't know what they mean. You don't know what they mean. Read them carefully, but then don't worry about them—just tell us about Bert." She had known Lance since before he was born. Given a glass of iced tea on the front porch, she could have regaled the listeners with heartwarming stories about Bert. And what would we on the prosecution team have done? Interrupted the saintly mother of the President in their hometown? What would that have looked like to Juror #6? Or anyone? I think not. We would have let her go on.

But this was not the front porch, there was no iced tea, and for whatever reason—time, opportunity, lack of understanding—she had not been adequately prepared by the defense. She came into court off an eighteen-hour flight from a humanitarian mission in Africa, looking elderly and frail, which she was. She took the stand, was asked these four gibberish questions, was clearly confused, gave four one-syllable answers, and she was done. They were out of questions. One of the news reporters in the room timed it: the saintly mother of the President of the United States, called in her own hometown, was on direct examination for only two and a half minutes.

To make matters worse for the defense, Marvin Loewy on the prosecution team *had* prepared Miss Lillian, in his own charming way. Marvin had stationed himself out in the hallway and waited for her to arrive. As she approached, he gave her his best smile, introduced himself, and told her that he worked for DOJ, and what an honor it was to work for her son the President. She smiled and said thank you, then headed into the courtroom, with Marvin right behind her.

When the defense so quickly exhausted their four questions, the judge asked if there was any cross from the government—expecting none. But Marvin stood up, smiled, and introduced himself again. And Miss Lillian smiled back, saying, "Oh, yes, Mr. Loewy," like they'd been friends for years. She had finally found a friend in this bizarre courtroom environment. Marvin thanked her for coming, Miss Lillian thanked him for having her, as if Marvin was the one who invited her, and that was it. No questions, thank you. So much for her impact as a witness for the defense.

It struck me then, and it strikes me now, that all of our witnesses are Miss Lillian. They all have a story to tell, but they've never told a story in the unnatural language and rhythm of question and answer. "Question, Pause, Answer, Stop!" We lawyers have to help them to understand just how different and difficult this is, and prepare them to navigate those strange waters. Miss Lillian was one of the several witnesses who showed me early in my career the importance of witness preparation, and I went on to write, speak, and practice extensively in the area. To this day, when I speak at continuing legal education (CLE) courses around the country, or when I get called in to help prepare a high-level or high-risk witness, I often tell that story. It helps people understand that they are not alone: the witness environment is an unnatural one for everybody and requires hard work and preparation.

"SPOT THE COW"

As trial lawyers, we believe in our cases, and we immerse ourselves in the documents and details. As it should be. The bigger or higher profile the case, the more time and effort we spend diving into it. As the size and profile of the case increases, so does the size of the trial team. A task force or large trial team works together, identifying more issues and materials, and reinforcing to each other the importance of each little detail. The result may be a masterpiece: a massive, detailed, carefully organized civil complaint or criminal indictment.

Therein lies the problem. Juror #6 has not drunk the Kool-Aid. He or she does not yet know whether the defendant is a bad actor, and therefore does not automatically assume that every document or detail demonstrates their evil. The more material we throw in, believing it's all important, the more likely we are to generate confusion, not outrage. There are various versions of the old saying, "When everything is important, nothing is important." Juror #6 needs to be convinced by as clear and simple a story as possible, not overwhelmed by a tidal wave of complexity. In every case, there comes a time when you have to go through the painful process of going at your masterpiece with a meat ax to reduce it to its persuasive essence.

But who wants to be the one to cut out that critical piece of evidence. In hindsight, if things go badly, a minor detail can come to be viewed as the missing smoking gun. If only we had left that in, the result would have been different.

Perhaps worse still, who wants to be the cheap shot artist: the lawyer who ignores the important issues and targets in a case to just pick the low-hanging fruit, to collect a quick stat. When I see or hear a trial lawyer brag about winning every case, I always wonder: does that mean they are exceptionally good, exceptionally lucky, or exceptionally afraid to bring tough cases? The need to simplify your case to tell a story that Juror #6 will understand does not mean cutting the heart out of your case, trivializing it to avoid what's important.

I was fortunate to learn those lessons in the first months of my career in the Lance case. I was not involved in the case until well after the indictment, so I do not mean to be critical of the great team that put it together. The investigation was a complex one, involving a number of different loans, banks, and alleged lies. The government team worked for months gathering facts and documents. At some point, in this and almost any investigation, you come to a fork in the road: Do you choose the big picture or focus on specific criminal actions? But in that kind of task force environment, everyone convinces each other that everything is important, and no one wants to be the one to take a meat ax to their collective creation.

The result, not surprisingly, was a lengthy, complicated, twelve-count bank fraud indictment brought in Lance's hometown of Atlanta. There were kernels of simplicity mixed in. For example, some fairly clear false statements to a bank in Chicago could have been charged as felonies up there—simply and separately—away from the complexity and away from the home cooking. Whether or not that was ever considered, it didn't happen, and the decision was made, and approved up the line, to bring the complex case in Atlanta.

The defense attacked and took full advantage of the complexity. They chipped away at the indictment in pretrial motions. At trial, they framed it as a battle between bureaucrats and their overly technical regulations on the one hand, and their "country banker" client and his deserving customers on the other hand. The simple false statements got buried in the complexity. All of which paved the way for their "country banker" to take the stand in his own defense and talk about "Spot the cow."

Lance took the stand and was at his friendly, folksy best. He said he became a banker to help people. His daddy had taught him that character was more important than collateral, pride was more important than paperwork. And that's how he had always done it. He would always remember one of his first loans, to an elderly local farm woman, Ethel, to buy a cow. Ethel fell behind on her monthly payments, and one day, when Lance was at his desk at the bank, Ethel walked into the bank, pulling the cow behind her.

"What are you doing?" Lance asked her.

"Mr. Lance," she replied, "I don't have the money for this month's loan payment, so I brought you Spot the cow."

Lance thought about it carefully, and said, "Ethel, you take Spot the cow home. You need that cow for milk. I believe in you, and I know you'll pay the loan back when you can." And sure enough, she did.

How do you fight Spot the cow with a 50-something-page legalese indictment? Through what was—if I recall correctly—a fourteen-week trial, we tried valiantly. But it wasn't enough. After a lengthy deliberation, the jury acquitted Lance on nine of the twelve counts and remained hung on the others. One of the counts they were divided on: false statements to a Chicago bank. To this day, I remain convinced that if the government team had chosen the other fork in the road, a simple false statement case in Chicago, Lance would have been a convicted felon.

It's not about missing key pieces or gutting the key parts of your case. It's about simplifying: paring it down to its essence. Telling a story that is simple enough that Juror #6 can understand it and care about it. Believe in your case, certainly, but don't let that belief interfere with crafting a case that is powerful and simple enough to persuade Juror #6. He or she will appreciate your having done so, and you are far more likely to appreciate the result.

5

U.S. v. Wallen

Executive Summary

Prosecution of the Department of Public Works (DPW) Commissioner of the City of Brockton, Massachusetts, for corruption.
As you read this chapter, be aware of:

- **Working up the ladder.** Crimes done in secret, between willing parties, are hard to prove.

- **This train runs on trust.** In every case, you have to search for ways to develop a bond of trust with each of your witnesses to get their true cooperation—and the truth.

- **"What we have here is a failure to communicate!"** The old line from the movie *Cool Hand Luke* is a challenge for witnesses. Communicating by question and answer is unnatural and difficult for the most articulate witnesses. Make any appropriate accommodations for those with language or other challenges.

U.S. v. WALLEN

Brockton is a city of about 100,000 people in southeastern Massachusetts, named after British General Isack Brock. The city has had its high points. It's sometimes referred to as the "City of Champions" because it was home to boxing legends Rocky Marciano and Marvin Hagler. It had a large shoe and leather industry, and, in fact, was America's largest producer of shoes during the Civil War. But legends fade, and the leather business went south and then overseas. Like other cities in the area, it has struggled with its economy, drugs, crime, and other problems, including corruption.

Frank Wallen was Brockton's Superintendent of Sewers, and then Commissioner of the Department of Public Works (DPW). In that position, he controlled the sewer, water, and highway departments—a large amount of outside contracting, digging ditches, and laying pipe, with little close supervision. Over time, it became known that you had to "pay to play" in Brockton: to get work from the DPW, you had to pay Frank Wallen. The Internal Revenue Service (IRS) began investigating. As an Assistant US Attorney in the Boston US Attorney's Office Public Corruption Unit, I was assigned to the case.

THE CHALLENGE OF CORRUPTION

The Wallen case is a good example of why corruption cases are so challenging to uncover, investigate, and prosecute. These crimes are different because they are usually done in secret, between consenting parties: consenting at least to the extent that, unlike a bank robber or other crimes, one party is not a victim at gunpoint, consenting at least to the extent that no one involved in the crime wants to get caught and all parties are similarly motivated to keep it quiet and hide their crimes. In a bribery case, that means hiding both the bribe and the reward. Uncovering them both, after the fact, can be very tough.

To investigate and prosecute, sometimes you have to work your way up the ladder: starting at the bottom and working your way up. If the target is a high-level public official, sometimes the lower rungs of the ladder are the private citizens or entities who paid the bribes. Get them to talk and you can start moving up the ladder.

These crimes are also different because they are usually not single incident crimes. They often start small, and then grow, fester, and explode. They draw people in, and then drag them deeper and deeper into the mud. A small favor becomes a larger favor, which becomes a small payment, which becomes a larger payment, and so on. Looking the other way on a contract becomes granting the contract, and more.

Such was the case with Frank Wallen. We believed that he was in corrupt relationships with a number of contractors, but our evidence and our case focused on one: Charm Construction.

Charm Construction was started by John Cardelli and Domenic D'Allesandro. They were, in many respects, the classic American success story. They arrived in the United States from Italy at seventeen years old with no money and found jobs digging ditches. They became known and respected as incredibly hard workers, got more jobs digging, and were able to scrape together enough money to buy an old pickup truck and start their own company, Charm Construction, digging water and sewer lines in the Brockton area.

Cardelli and D'Allesandro built their reputations and their company on hard work. But they soon learned that wasn't enough. If they wanted to do serious water and sewer work in Brockton, that path went through Frank Wallen. So, when Wallen started asking for small favors, a little work at his mother's house, helping his wife with a project—they agreed. Sure enough, over time the projects for Wallen got larger and larger, and added to the projects were cash payments, cars, and more. As the bribes became larger, so did the efforts to conceal them: phony invoices, false names, etc.

As the bribes became bigger, so did the benefits they received. Wallen explained various ways for them to cover some of the larger payoffs: inflated invoices, dummy change orders, additions to contracts, and more. Hard work only got them so far. They didn't like it, but they accepted it as the way it was—beyond their power to change. Eventually, the payoffs became so commonplace that the IRS got wind of it and started an investigation.

This leads to the other challenge of corruption cases: developing evidence. Before the investigation started, D'Allesandro had moved his family back to Italy (more on that later) and Cardelli was sick. The IRS built a tax case against Cardelli, and when we confronted him, he readily confessed to the bribes. He was to some extent relieved to get it off his chest. It had clearly been weighing on him all along.

But Cardelli's testimony by itself, even if he was well enough to testify at trial, which seemed doubtful, would not be enough. It would be one-on-one, from someone who had pleaded guilty to tax evasion—essentially lying to the IRS—against a distinguished public servant. It would not be enough for proof beyond a reasonable doubt.

The essential challenge of corruption cases: crimes done in secret, once they are no longer secret, are often lacking in hard, uncontroverted evidence. There are no innocent bank tellers, no fingerprints, no surveillance cameras, and in this case, given the passage of time and Cardelli's poor health, no tapes.

So we set out to do two things. First, the IRS went about trying to meticulously document and corroborate every favor, every project, every payment, and every effort to generate cash for the payments. Invoices, photos, bank records, workers, and more. Every word Cardelli said, we had to try to corroborate. Second, we had to try to corroborate him with another witness: Dominic, his former partner.

TRUST IS KEY

If you went out to a nearby park, sat on a bench next to a complete stranger, and started asking tough questions about their work, their lives, their finances, and their mistakes, what would happen? Most likely, they would think you were crazy, at best, and walk away. Why are we as lawyers so arrogant that we think we can do exactly that with someone just because they wear the hat of a witness? Ask strangers tough questions and expect them to tell us the truth? You can't. You have to work to develop a bond with a witness, to develop trust. Without trust, we're flying blind.

That can be a tough challenge in the best of circumstances; what about if the witness has left the country? Domenico D'Allesandro had come to this country at age seventeen and succeeded through hard work. Not only had he and Cardelli built Charm Construction into a large and successful company, but he had also married and started a family. America had delivered everything he had hoped for. But the lure of home and family—Italy—remained strong. America was wonderful, but he wanted to raise his children and grow old at home.

So before our investigation became known to him—having nothing to do with investigations, or Frank Wallen, or anything else—he sold his half of the business to Cardelli, sold his house, and moved back to the little village on Italy's Adriatic Coast where he had grown up. There, he bought a farm and, still the hard worker, was there every day farming and helping his neighbors and family. He became something like the unofficial mayor of the little town. Everyone knew him, everyone liked him.

Meanwhile, our investigation moved forward; we indicted both Cardelli and D'Alessandro for tax evasion, Cardelli pled guilty and cooperated, but D'Alessandro was gone. There was no way to bring him back. No one, the IRS folks assured me, had ever been extradited to the United States from Italy for tax evasion. It just wasn't taken that seriously there. Even if we tried it, the process could be dragged out for years. It wasn't going to happen. And without D'Alessandro, Wallen would likely get away with it. At best, it would be a very weak and risky case.

So I decided to go to Italy. At first, no one was buying it: "You're never going to get it approved in DC." "He's never going to agree to come back." "It's a waste of time and money." None of this was irrational. I would have to persuade D'Allesandro to meet with me, persuade him to return to the United States and plead guilty to tax evasion and risk prison, and persuade him to testify truthfully in an American courtroom about Frank Wallen. All true, I said, but if we didn't try, then Wallen probably walks, and that's just not acceptable. I persisted. I was a pain in the butt. Eventually, I got the OK.

Of course, nothing is that simple. I needed lots of things from lots of people:

- From the Department of Justice, I had to get agreement on what I could offer Domenic: a guilty plea to tax evasion and a recommendation of probation if he testified truthfully. But only a recommendation: The judge could still send him to jail.

- From the State Department, I had to get permission to go and a diplomatic passport: I was, after all, traveling on official business.

- From the IRS, I received insistence that its case agent go with me. That was OK, because I had a great case agent, but he had never traveled abroad, so he was going to be of limited help.

- From Domenic, I had to get his agreement to see me. When I was finally able to communicate my interest to him, he hired a lawyer in Boston to represent him, and we negotiated the date, time, and place of our meeting.

So Vince, the IRS case agent, and I flew from Boston to Rome, and then made our way to a train station for the train across Italy to the Adriatic Coast. From there we got to the little town where Domenic was living and met him for dinner. In Italy, as in other parts of the world, no serious business gets transacted until you have broken bread together. Food and wine come first.

We met for dinner in a small restaurant in the center of the little town. Everyone—owner, staff, and patrons—knew Domenic. He assured us that this was the best food in town, and then disappeared into the kitchen. We never saw a menu. Domenic spent ten to fifteen minutes back in the kitchen, talking with the chef, and then for the next four hours, we were treated to a procession of some of the best food and wine I've ever tasted.

There we were, four of us at the table. Domenic and I were directly across from each other, his lawyer on one side, the IRS agent on the other side, all enjoying the meal with the unwritten, unspoken rule: no business at the dinner table. We spoke of everything, except what we were there to speak about, and that was fine. It was a great dinner with great conversation, and getting to know each other. Slowly but surely, though, it evolved into a contest.

In my younger days, I had the blessing and curse of an extraordinarily high tolerance for alcohol. I could generally outlast most of my friends. Although that tolerance has diminished over the years, at the time of this dinner, it was still fairly high. Thank goodness. Slowly but surely, without a word being said about it, Domenic and I started matching each other on wine, glass for glass. Good food, good conversation, good wine—but matching glass for glass. It was personal. We knew we would be asking a lot of each other down the road, so we had to challenge each other, learn about each other, and trust each other.

I have no idea how many bottles of wine we drank that night, but it was a lot. Not only did we never see a menu, but we also never saw a bill—fortunately, because I'm quite sure we were exponentially beyond my government meal allowance. At some point, Domenic's lawyer and the IRS agent stopped trying to keep up, but Domenic and I kept at it. When we finally closed down the restaurant after this four- to five-hour dinner, the two of us were not just drinking companions but comrades in arms and trusted friends. Domenic and his lawyer went back to his house for the night, and the IRS agent and I stumbled to our hotel.

The next morning, the four of us met at Domenic's home. It was a wonderful place: a large, beautiful house on a working farm. Domenic gave us a brief tour of the grounds and then we went inside for coffee, which we badly needed after the night before, and to talk. My colleagues back in the US Attorney's Office, the IRS agent, and I had spent many hours strategizing about this negotiation. We knew that it was going to be a long and difficult process, probably over several days, with an uncertain outcome.

Domenic's US lawyer had told me before we went that he had explained to his client what his options were and what we wanted, and he didn't know if Domenic would agree. He doubted it. So I drank some coffee, settled into my chair, opened my file, looked at my notes, and cleared my throat to begin.

Domenic interrupted me. Negotiations, after all, are for strangers. Friends don't need those formalities; they work together based on trust. So he turned to his lawyer and said simply, "I trust Dan, work it out." It was over. And we did. Domenic would return to the United States, plead guilty to tax evasion, and testify, and I would recommend probation. It all happened so fast that Dominic's lawyer and I got back to Rome several days before our scheduled flights home and became fast friends enjoying two glorious days and long nights in Rome.

To everyone's surprise, Domenic came back to the United States, pled guilty, and testified. At his sentencing hearing, the judge pointedly asked Domenic if he understood that my recommendation of probation was only a recommendation and that if he pled guilty, the judge could still sentence him to jail. Domenic said he understood. The judge went on to say, in terms of rehabilitation, how impressed he was that Domenic had returned voluntarily. In terms of the seriousness of the offense, "I have in mind that tax evasion is somewhat of a national sport in Italy." That he also considered the importance of Domenic's testimony to the interests of justice here in the United States. He agreed with our recommendation and sentenced Dominic to probation, also allowing him to return to Italy after the trial.

Domenic worked hard with us to prepare for his testimony and was the key witness in the trial of Frank Wallen, He was credible and sympathetic, with a good memory of the facts despite his absence from the United States for several years. There was other evidence, to be sure, but we clearly would have had a tough time winning a conviction in this important case without his testimony.

Why did he come back? I was asked that question a lot before, during, and after the trial. Certainly, there were some specific reasons. He didn't want to have this hanging over him. He didn't want to be a "fugitive," even if in name only. He wanted to be able to bring his kids to visit friends and family in the United States without fear of being arrested. But I think the real answers were more profound. First, he truly wanted to do the right thing. He told me once, "I should never have let Frank do this to me. If he did it to me, he would do it to others."

Second, he was not putting his fate in the hands of a distant government bureaucrat, but with someone he believed in and trusted. Hour by hour, glass by glass, we had forged a bond that carried us through that challenging process together. You don't have to let every witness try to drink you under the table. In fact, I recommend against it. But in every case, you do have to find ways—and time—to forge a bond of trust with each witness.

Don't just try to sit down on that park bench and ask questions of a stranger. If you want the truth, work to develop a relationship that will bring it out. Thank you, Domenic, for your trust.

INTERPRETERS

Trial lawyers debate the pros and cons of using interpreters for witnesses in depositions or trial. Sometimes it's necessary: if the witness has little or no understanding of English, you may have no choice. But what if it's a close call? Some lawyers would prefer not to use interpreters if at all possible: it diminishes the connection between the witness and the lawyer, and between the witness and the finder of the fact. It just isn't worth it.

I disagree, and I learned that lesson in part from Domenic D'Allesandro. Domenic was born and raised in Italy. He came to this country at seventeen, and although he lived here for almost twenty years, he mostly lived, worked, and socialized with other Italian immigrants. So although he could usually get by in business, English never became his native tongue. Returning to Italy and living there for several years made the problem more acute.

Preparing for trial, Domenic resisted my suggestion that we get an interpreter. He was too proud. Sitting in a US courtroom with a jury and others watching him made using an interpreter too embarrassing. I tried to convince him without success. So we did a mock cross-examination without an interpreter to see how it would go. It didn't. It was a mess. He answered questions he didn't understand, answered questions that hadn't been asked, got confused, and—yes—got embarrassed. When it was over, he said let's get an interpreter.

The interpreter we brought in was a lovely lady. Smart, charming, she was petite and almost schoolmarmish in appearance, central casting for interpreters. I gave her the indictment and other materials to read so she could get familiar with the people and places in the case. She and Domenic spent time with us and became fast friends, which increased his comfort level with the decision.

At trial, she provided two important advantages. First, she helped Domenic understand what was being asked before he answered. Several times, particularly during my direct examination, Domenic answered questions without using the interpreter. Sometimes it worked, but sometimes it was clear that he had misunderstood part of the question. Fortunately, no real harm done, and during the breaks I kept encouraging him to use the interpreter as much as possible. Sometimes, when he ventured off on his own, the results were humorous and even endearing.

One example: Among the various bribes, Charm Construction bought several cars for the Wallen family. That included a big Buick Electra for Wallen's mother. In his testimony, I asked him why he bought the car, knowing that the answer was because Frank had told him to, in exchange for more contracts. But Domenic waved off the interpreter, and misunderstood the question to be not why *he bought* the car, but why *she wanted* the car.

So, with descriptive gestures, he replied, "She big woman (arms out wide), drive little s___t—box car (hands together)." The jury burst out laughing. I asked the question again a little more pointedly and got the right answer, so all was well. But it was a good indication of why interpreters are important, particularly for those subtle distinctions that can make or break your case.

Second, particularly on cross, the interpreter gave Domenic time and protection. On cross-examination, defense counsel asked questions aggressively and rapidly, trying to get some momentum going. Although his outrage was aimed at Domenic, the questions went first to this demure, petite woman. She would politely listen, then turn to Domenic and have a back-and-forth conversation in Italian, then turn back to the lawyer and give a polite, simple answer.

Sometimes the conversation between them was long, but the answer was short: turning to the lawyer after a long back and forth with

Domenic, and saying simply "No." Defense counsel complained to the judge, but the interpreter replied that interpreting the questions properly required some explanation, and that was the end of that. On the key government witness, defense counsel had a hard time building any momentum or intimidating the witness. The interpreter wouldn't let that happen.

After that experience, I have always tried to encourage the use of interpreters to try to minimize misunderstandings, in both directions. Obviously, it depends heavily on the quality of the interpreter, but that is just one more piece to test out and prepare for as you get ready for deposition or trial.

6

U.S. v. Anzalone

EXECUTIVE SUMMARY

Corruption investigation and prosecutions of City of Boston officials.

As you read this chapter, be aware of:

- **"The Blind Men and the Elephant":** In any case, it's important to push to find ways to tell the whole story, not just separate pieces.

- **Push for what is right:** There are often gaps in the law. As lawyers, we need to push for what is right, even if we miss in the short term.

- **Open their eyes:** Like all of us, jurors learn not just with their ears, but with all their senses. Don't sell your case short by not showing it to them through powerful demonstratives.

- **"In a conspiracy with the devil, there are no angels":** Some cases require lawyers to "work up the ladder," but that comes with both benefits and risks.

US v. ANZALONE

In the 1980s, I was part of the Public Corruption Unit of the U.S. Attorney's Office in Boston, which conducted an extensive investigation of the administration of Boston Mayor Kevin White. That investigation revealed widespread corruption and resulted in a number of convictions for bribery, extortion, fraud, and other crimes. Mayor White himself was never prosecuted, but the light was shone on corruption, which resulted in change and helped lead to a new mayor.

Ted Anzalone was Mayor White's right-hand man and, according to some reports, his bagman. We were told that to pay off the mayor, you went through Anzalone. So it was an important, high-profile step when we were able to bring a grand jury indictment against Anzalone for extortion and money laundering. We were getting closer.

TELLING THE WHOLE STORY

In any case, it's important to be able to tell the whole story, not just bits and pieces of it. Otherwise, the jury is left to struggle to understand the truth or with a distorted understanding. They become like the blind men in the ancient parable. A group of wise blind men come upon an elephant for the first time. Each touches a different part and comes to a different conclusion about what it is:

> One touches a leg and says, "It's a tree."
>
> One touches the trunk and says, "It's a snake."
>
> One touches an ear and says, "It's a fan."

And so on.

But sometimes the law makes it difficult to tell the whole story. That can create significant obstacles to reaching the truth. Take, for example, crimes committed in secret or involving cash, like drug dealing or corruption. After all, cash is cash. If a drug dealer has a bag of cash, how do you prove definitively that that cash came from drug dealing and not from under his father's mattress? Without a witness who was in the chain of custody of the cash, or other direct evidence, it can be a real challenge. It has to be done circumstantially and the strength of those inferences can vary. Keeping the story together can be essential to the case.

That was the challenge in Anzalone. We had one incident of extortion and two incidents of hiding cash or money laundering. But the evidence of extortion, a crime done in secret, came largely down to one witness, as it often does, so it was important to have the money laundering charges as evidence of the use of cash and efforts to hide it. On the other hand, the money laundering charges involved cash that Anzalone funneled to the mayor's mother and wife, not the mayor himself, so it was important to have the extortion charge to show motive to hide the cash.

We indicted the two crimes together and pushed hard to keep them together. The defense wisely tried to sever them. Judge Mazzone, the trial judge, was an excellent jurist, and we were hopeful he would understand the need to keep everything together. He did understand the need, but the law on severance made him uncomfortable. What evidence did we have, he asked, that the crimes were in fact linked together: essentially, that the extorted cash was the same as the laundered cash?

Cash is cash, we responded. There can never be a 100 percent link in a case like this. Many cases are tried successfully on circumstantial evidence, and the link should be a question of fact for the jury. They need to see the whole picture, not just have to blindly touch the elephant's leg. But Judge Mazzone didn't buy it. He felt that the evidentiary link needed to be stronger than it was, so he severed the extortion charge from the money laundering charges, ordering separate trials. We were devastated and angry.

We went ahead with two separate trials, with mixed results, as you'll see. We believe we were badly hurt by our inability to tell the whole story. Judge Mazzone ultimately agreed with us. Long after both trials were over, he told me in confidence that ordering the extortion and money laundering cases severed was one of the biggest mistakes he had made in his long and distinguished judicial career. Of course, by then, his change of mind was too late to do us any good.

"THE LAW IS AN ASS—OR IS IT?"

The money laundering charges against Anzalone were in two parts. The first was the "birthday party." Anzalone helped organize a birthday party for Mayor White's wife. But the State Ethics Commission discovered that among her "presents" were large numbers of checks for $1,000 from city employees. The Commission referred the matter to the U.S. Attorney's Office, and we started a grand jury investigation. One by one, we brought the gift-givers before the grand jury, and slowly, under the "pains and penalties of perjury," the truth came out. Later it came out at trial.

Most of the $1,000 gift-givers had actually never met the mayor's wife or only shook her hand at large gatherings. They were city employees, didn't make a great deal of money, and weren't wealthy. When pressed, they admitted that they had never given a gift anywhere close to $1,000 to anyone—spouses, children, family, whatever. Then we looked at their checking accounts—generally normal accounts without a big balance or big payments. In almost every case, there was a $1,000 cash deposit the day before they wrote their check for the same amount to the mayor's wife.

In the face of all this and more, the bad cover stories they had come up with started to crumble, and the truth came out. Anzalone, far above any of them in the city's power structure, had come to them, given each $1,000 cash, and told them to write checks to the mayor's wife. They did what they were told. Several times he had to tell them her first name— they didn't even know it. He did this over and over again. In this way, Anzalone was able to launder many thousands of dollars, from what we believe was illegal cash, to what looked like presents to the mayor's family.

Because of the severance, we couldn't tell the story, we couldn't say where we believed the money came from. So the defense didn't deny the scheme; they claimed they weren't hiding the money from the banks or the government. They were just hiding it from the nosy media. It is kind of a crazy theory, but they were helped by the lack of extortion evidence and the fact that the cash amounts were "only" $1,000 each, not close to the $10,000 reporting amount. It was enough to confuse the jury, and Anzalone was acquitted on this charge.

The second scheme was clearer. Banks are required to file a report with the government—a Currency Transaction Report (CTR)—for any cash transaction more than $10,000. Anzalone took $100,000 cash— which we believed was the proceeds of extortion—went to a local bank, and over about two weeks bought twelve cashier's checks (including three in one day), all under the $10,000 CTR limit. He then put the twelve checks back together and opened an account at a local invest- ment company in the name of the mayor's mother.

Clearly it was a scheme to structure a transaction to evade the reporting requirement to keep the cash hidden. There was no other explanation. This couldn't be legal. Unfortunately, the law at the time posed two obstacles.

First, when the Currency Transaction Reporting Act was passed, Congress extended its coverage to financial institutions *and* any other participant in the transaction. However, as the First Circuit put it, "for reasons known only to the Treasury Department, the regulation enacted by the Secretary . . . limited the reporting requirement to the financial institution *only*." Thus, Anzalone had no personal obligation to file a CTR.

Second, Congress, in its wisdom, apparently did not anticipate that people would simply structure transactions to avoid the CTR requirement. Thus, it did not include any provisions specifically outlawing structuring. There was a gap in the law wide enough to drive a Brinks truck full of cash through.

We were undaunted. Surely this kind of evasion couldn't be legal. Surely the law could not be that only the stupidest or laziest criminals, who didn't think to structure their transactions, would have to report. There's always more than one way to skin a cat. We indicted Anzalone using more general statutes: a scheme to conceal, aiding and abetting, and more. Other courts had called this a "sensible, substance—over—form approach." The US District Court agreed, rejected the defense's motion to dismiss, and we went to trial.

At trial, there was really no factual defense. The scheme was clear. Defense counsel pushed the legal argument, and we pushed back. In my closing argument, I said:

"So, the scheme becomes moving large amounts of cash through banks to make it appear legitimate . . . If this is all right, then the reporting requirement is meaningless. If you can simply create twelve phony transactions out of one large sum of cash, what's left of the law?"

And it worked. Anzalone was convicted of this scheme. The defense appealed.

In 1654, English playwright George Chapman coined the phrase "The law is an ass" in his play *Revenge For Honour.* It was repeated in 1838 by Charles Dickens in *Oliver Twist* and has become a common phrase. This prosecution was based on the premise that in this important area of the law, that old saying was *not* correct. The experienced trial judge agreed, the jury agreed, and then we went up to the First Circuit Court of Appeals.

Unfortunately, the First Circuit didn't really care if the law was an ass. The law is the law. I've argued before judges around the country, but I will never forget that argument. I stepped up to the podium, and before I could even begin, Judge Torruella leaned forward from the bench and sternly proclaimed: "Mr. Small, this is not Russia, we don't convict people of things that aren't crimes!" It was all downhill from there.

Whether prohibiting structuring was a "sensible . . . approach," whether allowing structuring made the law look like an ass, didn't concern the Court of Appeals. If Congress wanted to prohibit structuring, they could do so, and had to do it specifically. The Court of Appeals would not allow us to interpret the law this way. Anzalone's convictions were reversed. Two years later, Congress passed a law specifically prohibiting structuring a transaction to avoid the CTR requirement. If you look in the Congressional Record, 54 FR 28416-01, you will see a reference to *United States v. Anzalone*[1] as part of the problem Congress was trying to fix. I'm proud to say that there have been many successful structuring prosecutions since then. Anzalone should have been one of them, but the change in the law was too late to help us. Anzalone was a free man.

"SHOW AND TELL"

Any good teacher knows that students of any age do not learn best using only one sense—their ears. Law schools are among the few places where many teachers still think that long lectures are productive. At trial, a jury learns best using as many senses as possible, including:

Ears to listen;
Eyes to see:
Hands to hold.

As a result, one of the most important pieces of any trial strategy is powerful demonstratives. How do we show it, not just tell it. Demonstratives can leave an impression long after the jury has forgotten much of what was said. This is particularly true in a financial case where the

---

[1] 766 F2d 676 (1st Cir., 1985).

testimony can often be less than fascinating. So we worked on this in the Anzalone case. What would be most effective?

As I prepared to argue the case, I was drawn to the famous quote from Sir Walter Scott "Oh, what a tangled web we weave, when first we practice to deceive."[2]

I realized that's what we had here, a web of deceit, so we made a huge poster board demonstrative. On the left was a bag of cash with "$100,000" written on it, then lines diverged out from there to a middle column of images of the twelve cashier's checks, then lines went out from those twelve checks converging on a single pot of money on the right, with the name of the investment firm where they were all deposited. It really looked like a huge web. We put it up on an easel, and I stood in front of it to give my opening statement. We referred back to it in closing argument, saying that, "The web is obvious."

It was effective. The jury was clearly focused on it, and it helped to make the scheme clear. We as trial lawyers should always remember the importance—and power—of good demonstratives. They don't have to be complicated or fancy, just clear. And always be aware of them in the courtroom. In this trial, the very good defense counsel was so focused on giving its opening that it didn't realize that my big demonstrative was still up on the easel. I hadn't taken it down, and they neglected to do so. It remained up throughout their opening, and I saw the jury looking at our web of deceit at times during the defense opening. Lessons learned.

"DANGERS OF CLIMBING THE LADDER"

For crimes done in secret, like corruption or drug dealing, sometimes the only way to get to the top people is to climb up the ladder, one rung—one defendant—at a time. Catch someone lower down, and then pressure them to turn and testify against the next step up the ladder. George Collatos was a shining example of both the opportunities and dangers of this approach. He was also the key witness in our extortion case against Anzalone.

Collatos was a character. A sometimes con man, sometimes city employee. He had worked for the Boston Redevelopment Authority (BRA) and was a fundraiser for the mayor and a friend of Anzalone.

---

[2] Sir Walter Scott, *Marmion: A Tale of Flodden Field* (1808).

And a crook. The first step in his downfall was extorting cash from a building contractor wanting to do business with the BRA. Unfortunately for Collatos, the contractor was cooperating with the government. When the FBI moved in to arrest Collatos in the Dedham motel parking lot, where he had accepted the cash bribe, Collatos led them on a high-speed chase. The $12,500 in marked money was found in a ditch ten feet from Collatos' car at the end of the chase, and Collatos pled guilty to extortion and went to jail.

But the culture of omertà—of silence—was strong in the corrupt Boston administration at the time. The history was that corruption prosecutions were usually one-offs, where the government got its conviction and moved on. By contrast, if you kept your mouth shut, your friends in the administration would take care of you. Collatos was a prime example. Even though he had pleaded guilty to corrupting his public office to extort money, the Boston Retirement Board allowed him to keep his public pension. Thank you for your good service.

In the Public Corruption unit of the US Attorney's Office in Boston, we knew that we had to break that culture of silence. Corruption is rarely a one-time thing. We had no illusions that if we were lucky enough to catch someone taking a bribe, or paying a bribe, that was the only time it had happened. So, when we did catch someone and convict them, rather than let them go on their merry way when their case was done, we would subpoena them back to the grand jury and ask questions about other crimes.

Some people criticized this as unduly harsh or vindictive. After all, the person had been convicted and paid his dues. Leave the poor fellow alone. But generally, we weren't looking to revisit the conviction. We were looking for what *other* crimes and targets that defendant knew about. Nor were we looking for that defendant to incriminate himself. If the defendant refused to answer based on his Fifth Amendment right against self-incrimination, we would get an immunity order from the court, and compel him to testify.

What really scared the corrupt officials the most was the next step: when the defendant testified under court order, if they lied, we would seek to prosecute them for perjury. In a later corruption investigation, another former city of Boston official was caught on tape complaining about this. He whined: "Those guys at the US Attorney's office, they just don't give up!" To him, it was a complaint. To us, it was high praise.

George Collatos rode this process all the way through. After his extortion conviction, we brought him back into the grand jury and asked him about other illegal fundraising and other activities. First, he refused to answer under his Fifth Amendment rights. So we obtained a court order immunizing him and compelling his testimony. We brought him back into the grand jury, and again asked about other illegal activity. This time he lied and denied everything. Much of what he had done in the past we didn't have hard evidence of, so we could do nothing about some of his lies. But we were able to pull together enough hard evidence to charge him with twelve counts of perjury regarding illegal activities in Mayor White's administration and beyond.

Eventually, Collatos pleaded guilty to four of the perjury counts. So we brought him back yet again, and he finally started to tell us what he knew. Not everything, I suspect, but enough to be helpful. What he told us included the facts of Anzalone's extortion, so we moved forward to bring and build that case. The grand jury indicted Anzalone on extortion and the money laundering schemes described earlier.

But the successful process of moving up the ladder was also the problem. By the time Collatos became our key witness in the extortion case, he was already a convicted extortionist and perjurer. He had lied so much, even we weren't always sure whether he was lying or telling the truth, so we had to corroborate his testimony as much as possible with the efforts to hide cash and with other evidence. We also had to be up front with the jury that Collatos was a bad guy, but he was **Anzalone's** bad guy: his friend, collaborator, and fellow extortionist.

As discussed previously, with that framework, it was particularly devastating when one of the legs of that corroboration, the money laundering, was severed out of the case. We went forward, but it put that much more weight on Collatos' testimony. Too much weight. When we prepared Collatos for his testimony, we pushed hard to find out if there was anything else we needed to know, anything he wasn't telling us, but he assured us that all was well. It wasn't.

At trial, Collatos did reasonably well on our direct examination, but he seemed unusually nervous. On cross-examination, defense counsel got up, and with great drama asked: "Did you meet with Mr. Anzalone at La Bella's Coffee Shop and demand $200,000 to change your testimony?" There was a long pause, and then Collatos said, "I don't recall."

Memory is a funny thing. We remember some things but not others. When we prepare witnesses, including Collatos, we always tell them, if you don't remember, say so. This is not a memory test; there are always things that witnesses forget and that's OK. The jury understands. But this wasn't one of them. Sitting there at the government table, in shock on hearing this question, we knew as soon as there was a long pause—not an outraged denial—that it was true, that it had happened. His "I don't recall," answer after the long pause, just sealed it. Demanding $200,000 to change your testimony in a high-profile criminal case is just not something you're going to forget. It's one of those questions where "I don't recall" cannot be the right answer.

It turned out, the whole thing was a setup. Defense counsel set up the meeting at La Bella's and had several people hidden around the coffee shop to overhear the conversation. Collatos walked right into it. It was pretty clear that Collatos was offering to change his testimony to a lie, which, in a sense, corroborated the truth of what he said. But it didn't matter. A convicted extortionist and perjurer was now lying about his attempt to get money to change his testimony. It was too much for the jury. Whatever credibility Collatos might have had was gone, and Anzalone was acquitted.

Ironically, the only conviction that was upheld from the Anzalone case, was of Collatos. We simply could not let his attempt to sell his testimony, and his subsequent "I don't recall" perjury about it, stand. Collatos was indicted for perjury, went to trial, was convicted, and his conviction was upheld on appeal. To this day, it remains the only criminal case I know of where someone was convicted of perjury for answering "I don't recall." As the court said in upholding the conviction, "The content of that conversation formed the crux of Anzalone's defense." Some things you just don't forget.

7

U.S. v. Patriarca

Executive Summary

Investigation and prosecution of labor racketeering in Miami, Florida.

As you read this chapter, be aware of:

- **"Are you crazy?"**—It's difficult to get an expert to opine on future events, such as a defendant's health, and far more so when other factors intrude.

- **"Jurisdiction Is in the Eye of the Beholder"**—View jurisdiction as more than a technical hurdle. It can also be a turf issue, an ego issue, and an important part of the story you want to tell.

U.S. v. PATRIARCA

Raymond Patriarca was the powerful and ruthless boss of the Patriarca crime family in New England for more than three decades. His criminal history started in his teenage years, when he was charged with hijacking, armed robbery, assault, and more. At the ripe old age of twenty-five, he was indicted as an accessory to murder, and it went on from there. As he established control over the mob in New England, he ran his vast criminal empire from a very modest vending machine and pinball machine business in the Federal Hill neighborhood of Providence, Rhode Island. At one point, Patriarca was sent to jail for conspiracy to commit murder, but he continued to run his organization from prison, and continued when he got out.

The tentacles of Patriarca's criminal activity reached far and wide, including labor union offices. He allegedly worked with officials of the Laborers International Union to funnel the Union's insurance and service business into companies they had set up. They then allegedly looted the insurance premiums through kickbacks, payoffs and unearned salaries and fees, and improper personal expenses. As a federal prosecutor with the Department of Justice (DOJ)'s Organized Crime and Racketeering Strike Force, I presented the case to the grand jury and obtained the indictment.

EXPERTS

At the time of his indictment, Raymond Patriarca was seventy-three years old. He had some health and heart issues, like many men around that age, but was more than healthy enough to continue to rule his criminal empire with an iron hand. The joke among law enforcement was that Patriarca was in good health except for an allergy to courtrooms. He had used his age and health to try to avoid other court appearances, so it was no surprise that he would try the same thing with this federal indictment.

As you can imagine, after decades of doing special favors for his friends and grievous harm to his enemies, Patriarca had no problem finding a local doctor in Providence to say, "Oh dear, poor Raymond is too ill to go to trial!" The defense filed motions to keep him out of court. We could cross-examine the doctor with the fact that Patriarca was well enough to run a violent and extensive criminal enterprise, but once the issue was raised to the court, the government would likely need its own expert to counter their doctor. That's where things got difficult.

Expert witnesses are generally looking at things in hindsight: explaining and opining on what happened in the past, how something happened, what went wrong, etc. Experts often have differing opinions, and the judge or jury has to decide who is right and who is wrong. But the "wrong" expert generally still gets paid, and usually the only impact is on who gets what in the litigation. When the focus turns forward, toward the future, it gets a lot tougher. About 2,400 Americans die of heart-related problems every day. Many of them seemed perfectly healthy the day before. How far can a doctor go to give the court certainty—or even comfort—that it won't happen here?

Two basic truths collided. First, criminal trials are stressful events for all concerned, including the defendant, maybe even for a seasoned pro like Raymond Patriarca. Second, doctors are not fortune tellers; they generally cannot predict the future with certainty. So, for a doctor to take the witness stand and say with certainty that a seventy-three-year-old man will not have his health impacted by the stress of a criminal trial, is a tall order even under the best of circumstances.

These were not the best of circumstances. I searched for doctors with good reputations, who could examine the defendant and then report to the court with a clean bill of health for trial. Then I started the process of interviewing them. One after the other, they were interested in being an expert witness for the government—until I mentioned the name of the defendant. Then every one of them lost interest. Some of them communicated that politely, with a simple, "No, thanks." Some were more vocal: "Do you think I'm crazy? Hell no!"

It's a tough sell in the abstract. But when we layered on the reality of Patriarca's violent history and reputation, it became impossible. Doctors told me they feared for their business, their houses, their lives, and their families. It was no longer just a matter of someone winning or losing the litigation. It was personal. As a lawyer prosecuting Patriarca for racketeering, I was in no position to absolutely deny the danger—however uncertain.

Without a strong medical expert, we couldn't get Patriarca to trial. He was severed out of the case, and it went forward against the other defendants. It was still a prominent case, including high union officials, but not the case we had intended and hoped for. Who knows, maybe the experts were right to be reluctant, or maybe it was just his time: after continuing to run the mob for another three years, Patriarca eventually died of a heart attack. He is buried in Gate of Heaven Cemetery in East Providence, Rhode Island.

"JURISDICTION IS IN THE EYE OF THE BEHOLDER"

In truth, my initial assignment from the chief of the Organized Crime and Racketeering Strike Force on the Patriarca case was more complicated than the usual "go see what's happening." The underlying actions in the case had happened in Rhode Island and Florida, but mostly Rhode Island. Despite it being potentially high profile, for various bureaucratic and other reasons, the case had bounced back and forth between Providence and Miami, until someone realized that all that bouncing had brought the case perilously close to the five-year statute of limitations. Imagine how embarrassing it would be if a potentially high-profile case was bounced, bungled, and delayed out of existence.

So my assignment was more pointed than usual. Basically, it was: (1) find out where the files are currently, (2) go there and assemble the team, (3) decide if there is a case, and (4) get it before a grand jury and indicted fast, before it disappears! Get on a plane and make it happen. So I did.

For reasons I never quite figured out, the files were in Miami and some of the initial leg work had been started there. I thought about boxing everything up and moving it all back to Providence, Rhode Island, where the case probably belonged, but time was short, and it was quicker to get the Federal Bureau of Investigation (FBI) team who knew the case best on a plane from Providence to Miami. Once assembled, we very quickly reviewed the case, drafted an indictment and a memo to go up the line recommending prosecution, got it approved in Washington, brought it before a grand jury in Miami, and got the indictment. That's when it got even more complicated.

Federal judges are busy people, and over time they learn to be very protective of their dockets. The judge to whom this case was assigned had been on the bench for some time and had become notoriously protective. He looked at our indictment and quickly decided that even if we had enough of a Miami link legally, at least factually, it really should have been brought in Rhode Island. It was a Rhode Island case. Why was it clogging up his docket in Miami? From the beginning, that was his view of the case. It was just not his problem.

Grand jury indictments are given great deference by the courts. A panel of citizens has assembled, heard evidence, and voted to bring (or "return") an indictment, based upon probable cause—a much lower standard than a criminal trial's proof beyond a reasonable doubt. Indictments are generally written by prosecutors for the grand jury's review with an eye toward presenting the evidence persuasively, making sure that all the legal requirements are met, and that the case can get to a trial jury.

Given all that, motions to dismiss an indictment are rarely brought and very rarely successful. Yet in this case, we knew that the judge didn't want this case in front of him in Miami, so we were concerned. Sure enough, the defense filed a motion to dismiss, primarily on statute of limitations grounds. We knew that we were close but believed we were on solid ground. However, the judge found a way to get the case out of his courtroom, ruling that the Racketeer Influenced and Corrupt Organizations Act (RICO) conspiracy statute required overt acts, and the one overt act we had alleged in the indictment within the statute of limitations wasn't good enough. Case dismissed.

We appealed to the Eleventh Circuit. In my argument to the Court of Appeals, I emphasized the importance of the case, and whether or not Miami was the best venue for the case, it was a legally sufficient one and we were within the statute of limitations. The Court of Appeals agreed, making the law clear that overt acts didn't need to be specifically alleged in a RICO conspiracy indictment, that the indictment clearly alleged a crime within the statute, and reversed the District Court's dismissal.

In many federal jurisdictions, if a case goes on appeal from the District Court and then comes back, it goes to a different judge so there can be no allegation of bias or retribution. Alas, there was no such rule in the Southern District of Florida at the time, so the case went back to the same judge who believed it should be gone in the first place. He was a gentleman about being reversed but was clearly unhappy.

Meanwhile, more than two years had gone by between the indictment and the Court of Appeals decision. I had moved on to a new job with the Public Corruption Unit of the US Attorney's Office up in Boston and was too caught up in other matters there to leave for the time it would take to prepare and try the case in Miami. Another team was assigned to the case from the DOJ in Washington, DC.

I felt bad for them. They were walking into a problem that was not of their making: trying a case in front of a judge who believed it should not be there and that we had gotten his decision reversed by the Court of Appeals. No judge likes their decisions to be reversed, so it was a double whammy. He was exerting control over his docket—his turf—which is not completely unreasonable, and we had challenged him and won. Sure enough, when the case went to trial, the judge waited impatiently through the government's case and then dismissed the case—again— this time in a way that made it virtually impossible to appeal. It was over.

Patriarca had avoided trial based on his health claims, and the labor union officials had the charges against them dismissed. The government had lost all around.

In retrospect, perhaps we were too focused on the legalities and logistics, not on the people and places. We believed that we had enough legal and factual basis to bring the case in Miami, therefore it was not worth the mad dash up to Rhode Island. But in every case, you are telling a story. You want to do everything you can to make sure that your audience wants to hear it. Of course, we didn't know which judge would draw the case before we brought the indictment in Miami, and certainly there were other judges who would not have been as upset about the location issue. But who knows: maybe other judges would have been even more upset. Do everything you can to find the right audience for your story. In retrospect, I probably should have thrown everything in boxes, raced to the airport, and brought the case in Rhode Island. Lessons learned.

8

U.S. v. Rendle

EXECUTIVE SUMMARY

Prosecution of U.S. Department of Housing and Urban Development (HUD) officials for corruption in a program for low-income housing.

As you read this chapter, be aware of:

- **Understanding the media**—For many clients and cases, there are valid interests that go beyond the four walls of the courtroom. Sometimes, it's important to understand and be comfortable in the court of public opinion.

- **Respect, respect, respect**: Productive relationships with all players in the litigation world start with respect. Judges are no exception. Work to develop mutual respect.

- **Reading the room**: Don't get so caught up in your own advocacy that you lose sight of where you are, what's going on around you, and how people are reacting.

- **Tragedy in trial**—Many trials have an element of tragedy. Be aware of and sensitive to that, but don't let it distract you too far from your job of doing the right thing.

U.S. v. RENDLE

The HUD 518-B program was designed to provide assistance for needed renovations for low-income housing. It was a good program—if it's done right. But in Massachusetts, some of the folks who ran the program were doing it wrong: taking bribes from building contractors in exchange for giving out 518-B contracts. You name it, they demanded it. Not just cash, but roofs, siding, renovations, all kinds of work on the homes of HUD officials and their families.

In the Public Corruption Unit of the US Attorney's Office in Boston, HUD investigators complained that the program was corrupt. We called in a large number of the contractors, the word would get out, and one by one I gave them my "train speech": "The train is leaving the station, and you can either be on it or under it, makes no difference to me!" Mostly it was a bluff: we believed they were making payoffs, but we really didn't have enough hard evidence yet. But the bluff worked. One of the contractors, plagued by guilt and fear, gave in, confessed, and agreed to plead guilty and cooperate. Once he did, other dominoes started to fall, and we obtained solid testimony against several HUD officials, which we then did everything we could to corroborate with documents and other evidence.

Ultimately we were able to bring an indictment against ten people, including six present or former HUD officials. The case moved forward towards trial and I was fortunate to persuade the Public Integrity Unit of the Department of Justice (DOJ) in Washington, DC, to send one of its top trial lawyers up to assist: my good friend Jim Cole, who I had started with at the DOJ and had remained there when I went up to Boston, where he was later to go on to fame and fortune. Trying a case with a partner can be tricky. Trying it with one of my best friends, and a great trial lawyer, was an extra treat.

UNDERSTANDING THE MEDIA

Many lawyers are not comfortable with the media: they don't like reporters, don't trust them, or just have not had any experience (much less good experience) dealing with them. So they ignore the press and hide behind the old saying that, "We don't try our cases in the media." That's fine for many cases, but for many others, it misses the point. All kinds of cases—criminal and civil—are brought for reasons that go beyond just winning or losing one case in court. In all kinds of cases, our clients—whether an individual, a company, or the government—have interests beyond the verdict itself. Deterrence, reputation, profits, sending a message of some kind, educating the public: there are many reasons why the megaphone of the media can help to reach broader goals.

In a high-profile case, we often don't have to seek out or generate media interest. It's already there. Our job as trial lawyers is to inform and shape that interest. Many reporters don't have the background, knowledge, or experience to fully understand what a case is about or what is happening in court. Indeed, it's not unusual when trying a high-profile case to see a media report of a trial day and wonder if the reporter was really in the same courtroom, as the report is so far from reality.

I was fortunate in this respect. I had a variety of jobs before, during, and after law school that brought me in contact with the media. I knew reporters personally, was friends with some, and had some understanding of both the challenges they face in reporting legal cases and the opportunities they present to trial lawyers.

All of this is exponentially true in corruption cases. They are naturally of interest to the media. From the prosecution's perspective, the government is never going to uncover and prosecute all corruption. So it's important that the cases that are brought be reported positively and widely, both as deterrence to those who might be tempted by corruption and as reassurance to the public that something is being done. From the defense perspective, if the client is a public official, how the public sees them through the lens of the media may be particularly important to them. A lifetime of building a public image or reputation may be at stake.

One of the things that lawyers often don't understand, is that reporters—and their bosses—are competing with each other. Competing to be the first, to be the best, to get the "scoop," to get the good stuff. Whether the goal is ratings and the advertising dollars that result, or awards and recognition, or just ego, it can be a tough business. Boston before the internet was a good example: There were two major newspapers, *The Globe* and *The Herald*. The media environment now is far more diffused and newspapers no longer dominate, but back then it seemed like everyone read one or the other. On a train, plane, bus, whatever, everyone was reading a newspaper, just like now we're all looking at our devices. As a result, the two papers competed intensely for stories.

The Rendle case was an attractive one for the media. After all, these HUD officials were supposed to be running a program to help low-income families whose houses were falling apart. Instead, they were using it to line their pockets. The renovations on the officials' homes were usually much nicer than anything the contractors were doing for those they were supposed to be helping.

We understood the attractiveness of the case and the value of using it to get the word out about our efforts to fight corruption. Some indictments are just bare-bones legal documents. The indictment in this case was much more: we used the evidence we had to try to explain the program and its abuse, and to tell the story clearly and dramatically. Same with the initial hearing, when the indictment was made public: we used the public event to tell the story. It worked: The media was intrigued.

But I forgot about the competition part. Both major newspapers, *The Globe* and *The Herald*, had reporters assigned to cover the federal court in Boston. I knew them both from prior cases, and from being around the courts and the places court people hang out at the end of the day. Like all the media, both reporters were interested in the case and attended the hearing. When it was done, as I was walking out of the courtroom, *The Herald* reporter was walking with me and chatting about what a great case this was. I agreed, and commented that it was sort of, "like Robin Hood in reverse." They were taking from the poor to give to the rich. We said goodnight and went our separate ways. I thought nothing of it.

Until the next morning. Both papers featured the story on the front page. But in *The Herald*, above the banner headline, was the quote: "Robin Hood in Reverse," and the article below noted me as the source for the quote. My first reaction was delight—look at the cool quote on the front page! But when I got to the office that morning, the reporter for *The Globe* had already called several times. He was furious. And his editor had called my boss, the US Attorney, equally angry.

"How could you do that to me?" *The Globe* reporter asked angrily when I returned his call. "You didn't say that in the open hearing, why would you feed such a great line just to *The Herald?* That's not fair! You're not playing by the rules!" And he was right. Our job as lawyers is to speak to the court, their job as reporters is to report on what is said and written in open court, or in another environment that gives equal access. We shouldn't be favoring one media outlet over another by feeding them an exclusive quote. That wasn't my intent: after an exhausting day in court, I thought I was just chatting with a friend. But I didn't make that clear, and it dramatically demonstrated the need for clarity and caution in dealing with the media. The next time I saw *The Globe* reporter at the bar where the courthouse regulars hung out, I bought the first couple rounds. Lessons learned.

RESPECT, RESPECT, RESPECT

In federal criminal cases, judges are drawn for the case at random. For the Rendle case, we drew a "T," which was a cause for distress to many in the US Attorney's Office in Boston. Judge Joseph Tauro (the "T") was smart and experienced but widely viewed as notoriously pro-defense. Indeed, it felt like I had seen him threaten to throw more government agents and prosecutors in jail, than defendants. He also didn't like the law of conspiracy and was not a big believer in prosecuting white-collar crime. For many in the US Attorney's Office, to draw a "T" on a case was a scary and depressing event. A bad way to start a case.

Yet I liked him, respected him, and had had success in front of him in the very kinds of conspiracy and white-collar crime cases he was viewed as opposing. It got to the point where if other Assistant US Attorneys in the office drew a "T," some of them would come to me for advice to learn my "secret" for surviving in his courtroom. I had to think about it, understand it, and try to explain it.

The "secret" was respect. Mutual respect. It sounds simple but it's not. The first piece was preparation. Judge Tauro so dominated his courtroom, and so favored the defense, that many prosecutors wondered what was the point of spending all those hours preparing—he was just going to do whatever he wanted. Sometimes that was true and unavoidable, but the reality was, in that courtroom, you had to be doubly prepared. Judge Tauro had to understand that you knew the case and the law. If he was too quick to jump to conclusions, you could see through it and respond, and your response would be thoughtful and well-supported, not based on emotion or bias—or fear.

This leads to the second piece—judgment. Too often, prosecutors would allow their negative impressions of Judge Tauro to control their actions in his court. They would gravitate to one extreme or another: fighting him on everything or rolling over and giving in on everything.

But neither extreme works, because neither extreme shows respect or deserves respect.

You can't try to fight every battle to the bitter end. You're an advocate. You take positions you believe in. But those positions may not be the only way to look at the issue. So you have to make your arguments but then pick your battles. If everything is important, then nothing is important. If you fight every battle, are you standing up for principles or just indicating that you don't know which principles are worth fighting for? Judge Tauro—and most judges—respected a strongly held position, but less so someone who holds every position equally strongly.

The other extreme was no better. If you roll over and give up too easily, why are you making the argument in the first place? If you don't think it's important, why are you wasting the judge's time? Besides, it's no fun for anyone—even a judge—to "win" an argument with someone who isn't pushing back. Rolling over isn't respecting the judge or yourself.

I would make sure that I always came to Judge Tauro's court prepared on the facts and the law, and also prepared to pick my battles. Over time he grew to respect that, and I grew to respect him for it. Sometimes he would agree with me, sometimes he would rule against me, and sometimes we would go at it. At one motion hearing in the Rendle case—alas, I have long since forgotten what the issue was—there was a motion that I felt strongly about and so did he . . . but in the other direction.

So we went at it. Vociferously. Voices raised. The full courtroom of onlookers—mostly lawyers waiting for their cases to be called—was shocked, convinced that at any moment, he was going to have the US Marshals handcuff me and send me off to jail for contempt. No prosecutor argued with Judge Tauro like that and survived. Had I gone mad? But we had built a relationship of respect, and on some level, he enjoyed the battle. Finally, before things went off the rails, he stopped me and said, "Look, I understand your position, I know you hold it in good faith, but I disagree with it! Move on!" So I did. One battle lost but respect gained on both sides. Survived to fight another day. Lessons learned.

Respect, by the way, applies to all players in the litigation environment. It amazes me when I see lawyers sucking up to judges but then ignoring—or worse, being rude to—all the other players: clerks, court reporters, court officers, etc. How much extra effort does it really take to be nice to everyone in the building? That effort can be well worth it in a hundred ways—small and large. One trial lawyer friend had a sign on his office wall that said, "Judges can hurt you. Clerks can kill you!" Truer words were never spoken. Everyone in court has a job to do. Show respect all around. It's the right thing to do, and it might just save you from disaster one day.

READING THE ROOM

As trial lawyers, we are advocates, but we cannot let our strongly held beliefs blind us to the realities of the courtroom. Our clients—whether individuals or the government—need counsel who can "read the room": The judge, the jury, the atmosphere, the direction things are going. It can be a challenge to step back from our advocacy long enough, and far enough, to really read the room.

One extreme example from a different case and a different judge: As an Assistant U.S. Attorney in Boston, I prosecuted a U.S. Customs agent for stealing and selling confidential information from the U.S. Customs computer system. He hired an experienced criminal defense lawyer to represent him. This lawyer was known for attacking the government: the government had overreached, made mistakes, acted improperly, etc. That was helpful to the defense in some cases, but how does it help to say the government is bad when you're defending a government agent?

It didn't. The jury was confused but not convinced by the lawyer's attacks. The judge—a conservative judge for that district—was unsympathetic and impatient. The attacks were unsuccessful, and the defendant was convicted on both charged counts. Then, at sentencing, it got worse. As the prosecutor, I got up first and talked about the importance of the confidentiality of the Customs system and the seriousness of the agent's breach of trust. I argued for a sentence on each count but said that the sentences could run concurrently, as was common practice—not stacked on top of each other, consecutively. Then it was the defense's turn.

Most of the time, for the defense, the sentencing hearing is a time for groveling. Your trial defenses haven't worked, questions of guilt or innocence have been resolved against you, and the judge needs to hear remorse and pleading for leniency, from both lawyer and client. All the more so for a corrupt law enforcement officer, appearing for sentencing before a conservative judge. Courtroom etiquette doesn't allow you to get down on your knees to beg—but if you could, you would.

Not here, not this time. This defense counsel was so caught up with his constant refrain that he got up at the sentencing hearing and railed against the government again. Everyone in the courtroom was shocked. That ship had sailed: this was not the time or place for that argument. Read the room. He didn't, and when he was done, the judge was clearly angry. He glared at the defense counsel while he announced that he was accepting the government's sentencing recommendations on both counts. And then he paused, and still glaring directly at the defense counsel, said that the sentences on the two counts would run **consecutively**, not concurrently as I had recommended, effectively doubling my recommendation. We'll never know what sentence the judge would have handed down if the defense counsel had done a better job of reading the room, but I am convinced that his failure to do so cost his client time in prison.

In the Rendle case, the importance of reading the room started early. Judge Tauro and I disagreed on many things but we agreed on one: we both loved trials—the excitement, the entertainment, the challenges. That can sometimes be difficult to maintain in a complex, multiple-defendant, white-collar case (in Rendle, if memory serves me correctly, six or seven defendants went to trial together), but it remained no less important.

Our first witness at trial was not intended to be exciting. This was the beginning of what was to be a month-long trial. We had explained in opening that we would call a HUD auditor first, just to explain the housing program and how things worked. Dull, but necessary to lay the foundation for what was to follow. Our witness was right out of central casting for auditors: smart, soft-spoken, and (I say this with fondness and respect) boring. He did a good job of explaining the program, and then I sat down.

Cross-examination of the auditor probably should have been limited or nonexistent. Nothing he said was disputed, he had no personal knowledge or involvement with the defendants, mostly just what he had learned from reading the HUD and case documents, and most of that, coming out of his mouth, would be hearsay. "No questions" would have been a very effective cross-examination, as it often is. But the lawyers—and their clients—were impatient, wanting to do something to counter the wave of evidence they knew was coming. So, one after another, defense counsel tried to use this poor auditor to put forward their defense theories, some of the lawyers cross-examining him for longer than he had been on direct, and in directions we hadn't touched on in his direct examination.

He was the wrong witness for their purpose. Clearly a nice fellow, clearly just an auditor, not evil, and not able to make their theories come to life. They should have seen it and stopped. I objected at various times on speculation, lack of foundation, and hearsay, but not too vehemently, and Judge Tauro overruled most of my objections. He was giving the defense great leeway, but I could see him getting more and more impatient, as this unsuccessful effort droned on. In an interesting corruption case, they had managed to both bore and confuse the judge and the jury, whose time and attention the judge protects vigorously.

Finally, the last defense counsel ran out of steam. Most of the time, redirect examination is short, limited to the direct examination, and restricted to nonleading questions. But reading the room, I felt more was needed, and possible. I gathered all the energy I could, jumped to my feet, and dramatically launched into essentially our closing argument in question-and-answer form. Leading, raising my voice, and going far beyond what we had done on direct. The witness wasn't quite sure what was happening, but bravely hung on for the ride.

Defense counsel, of course, went crazy: objecting to hearsay, scope, and everything else, just like I had during their cross-examination. But they had misread the room. After a long pointless slog through cross-examination, we were back to what we hoped—and Judge Tauro believed—trials should be: fast-paced, informative, and entertaining, and Judge Tauro was pleased. He sternly overruled their objections. Finally, after one objection, he glared at the defense counsel and said, "You opened this door, you have to eat whatever crawls out of it!" After a redirect that was twice as long as the direct, I sat down a happy man, having delivered our closing argument through our first witness, a simple auditor. The auditor, by the way, was a great guy, and later thanked me for a fun ride.

Meanwhile, it got worse for the defense. After the auditor was finished, Judge Tauro called all counsel to the sidebar. The defense counsel was excited: sidebar conferences in that courtroom often included Judge Tauro berating the government. Surely, he was going to rein me in after that extraordinary redirect. Instead, to everyone's shock, Tauro turned to the defense counsel and said, "Is that the best you have? Am I listening to a month-long sentencing hearing?" And he told a stunned group of lawyers—on both sides—that he was sending the jury home for the day to give us time to work out guilty pleas.

We started a round-robin set of plea negotiations with each of the different defense counsels. At one point, negotiations broke down, because counsel thought I was being too tough on their clients. I said fine, let's go back to trial. Instead, they asked for a conference with the judge. We had all seen Judge Tauro strongarm prosecutors into more lenient plea deals. Not this time. Judge Tauro heard them out, and then said, "I think Mr. Small has a very strong position, I can't disagree with him here." And sent us back to work. Eventually, all of the defendants pled guilty to serious crimes, except the one most minor defendant, who we severed out to deal with later.

Reading the room is important in many situations but particularly so in a trial. What's needed and not. What's appropriate and not. Where things are going. We have to be carefully tuned into the room and the people around us, and not so focused on our own case and our own words that we lose the room.

TRAGEDY IN TRIAL

Trials are serious matters. Many trials—civil or criminal—have an element of tragedy in them. Someone is going to lose, and the consequences can be devastating. Most people are not all bad. So even if the punishment fits the crime, it's still tough: on them, on their future, on their family, and more. Such was the case here. George Rendle, the lead HUD inspector defendant and the most corrupt, had been a respected member of the community. Nice house, good job, nice family, all the trimmings.

Then, with the indictment and the media coverage, it all came crashing down—suddenly and dramatically. His picture was in the paper, the good program he helped manage became a code name for corruption, and even the houses he owned and was proud of became exhibits in the case against him since work done on them had been among the bribes. He reacted badly, and it started him on a downward spiral.

First, Rendle created some phony documents to support his defense. We discovered the scheme, and it only added obstruction of justice charges to his mounting problems. Next, he hired counsel and loudly proclaimed his innocence, but the evidence against him continued to mount. He was out of a job and the money he spent on counsel was never coming back. Next, his counsel apparently assured him that they had a defense-friendly judge. During our plea negotiations, as I said, they went back to Judge Tauro to get him to push me to be more reasonable: first on what charges Rendle would plead guilty to, and then to try to avoid a jail sentence. But Tauro had heard enough: both times, to their surprise and dismay, he turned them down and sent us back to work.

At sentencing, Judge Tauro sentenced Rendle to a prison term. In a violent crime case, generally once someone is sentenced to jail, they go right to jail (if they're not already there). But white collar was still viewed differently. As was common practice back then in white-collar cases, his lawyers asked that he be allowed out on bail for a short period (I think it was 30 or 60 days) to "settle his affairs" before reporting to prison. I argued against it. I told Judge Tauro that Rendle had been on a downward spiral that may have reached the point of desperation. I didn't know what he would do, but I was deeply concerned: for my witnesses, that he might flee, for himself and his family. But Tauro was sympathetic to his plight and granted his request.

Despite my concerns, none of us really saw it coming. On the night before he was to report to prison, Rendle went out to the enclosed garage at his home, got into his car, turned it on, took a bunch of sleeping pills, and slept until he died of carbon monoxide poisoning from breathing the exhaust. Worse still, what Rendle clearly didn't realize was that there was an open vent between the garage and the house, where his wife and mother-in-law were sleeping. The carbon monoxide went through the vent, into the house, and killed them both in their sleep, as well.

The news of this next morning put us all in shock. I sat in my office for some time, not sure what to do. Eventually, someone reminded me that I had a hearing on another case, in front of another judge. I wandered up to court, still somewhat in a fog, and did my best to conduct whatever hearing it was—I've long since forgotten.

Every day, the clerk's office printed up a list of proceedings before each of the federal judges, which often included the names of counsel for each side. Judge Tauro, having heard the news of the deaths, apparently looked at the list, saw which courtroom I was appearing in, and sent his clerk to ask me to come see him in his chambers right away. I had no idea why the judge was calling for me, and I viewed the request with great trepidation. But when a federal judge summons you, "no thanks" is not an option.

There was no reason for my fears. We all have roles to play in court, but sometimes, the human side of life overcomes those roles. This was one of those times. Judge Tauro invited me into his chambers, sat me down, and gave me a lecture that was both stern and heartwarming that I will always remember with gratitude. "This was not your fault," he said. "You have an important job to do as a prosecutor, and you did it well. Always remember that. We can argue whether I should have granted your request and sent him right to jail, but that's for another day. He did a crazy and terrible thing. None of us saw this coming, and none of this should change your commitment to doing and saying the right thing. Now go back, apologize to Judge Mazzone that I pulled you out of his courtroom, and keep doing what you're doing!"

That was it. What an extraordinary thing for him to do. He was done. And he was right. So I went back to court, and the fog of guilt that had enshrouded me all morning lifted somewhat. Not entirely. We cannot control everything that goes on around us. Tragedy is a frequent companion in litigation and life. But we can control our determination to keep doing the right thing and doing it as well as we can. Lessons learned.

9

John D. Gilbert

EXECUTIVE SUMMARY

Defending a naval architect in a civil negligence suit brought by the owner of a fishing boat.

As you read this chapter, be aware of:

- **Core themes:** Develop your core themes by talking to nonlawyers about your case, and then search for ways to bring them to life for the jury.
- **The lawyer is the captain of the ship:** The trial lawyer has to become an expert, dive into the issues, and not cede control of your case to the experts.

INTRODUCTION

Jack Gilbert was widely known as one of the top naval architects on the eastern seaboard. He designed much of the East Coast fishing fleet and, as that work slowed or went overseas, broadened out to designing ferries, tugboats, fireboats, and many other commercial vessels. One of the fishing vessels he designed, we will call it the *Bailey*, was a beautiful ninety-three-foot working boat. However, when it went to sea, its owner complained that it showed signs of instability, and he brought a lawsuit against Jack for negligence in the United States District Court in Portland, Maine. I was retained to help represent Jack in defending the suit. He was a great naval architect and became a good friend.

The Grand Banks is a large area of the Atlantic Ocean southeast of Newfoundland. It is called the "banks" because its submerged highlands create a relatively shallow bank, ranging from 80 to 330 feet. There, the cold Labrador Current mixes with the warm waters of the Gulf Stream. That turbulence lifts nutrients to the surface and creates one of the richest fishing grounds in the world. English explorer John Cabot discovered this extraordinary fishing area in 1497, sailing his boat the *Matthew*, and it has been a major resource for fishing fleets from around the world ever since.

However, the same turbulence that creates extraordinary fishing also helps create extraordinary weather. It can be an inhospitable environment, with rogue waves, fog, icebergs, winter storms, hurricanes, and sea ice. Designing a boat for those conditions is a challenge. So was bringing them to life for a jury. Take winter ice, for example. The jury may hear that term and conjure up visions of cute little icicles, hanging from the rigging.

In reality, there's nothing cute about winter ice to these fishing crews. In temperatures far below freezing, the spray from the sea below, and the rain, sleet, and snow from the skies above, accumulate ice on every surface, every support, every line, and not in cute little icicles but in rapidly growing thick sheets. A fishing boat this size can accumulate thousands of pounds of ice above the waterline. All that added weight can create a serious threat to the boat's stability and the lives of all aboard.

To try to keep control over winter ice, a crewman may be assigned, often at all hours of the day and night, and in the worst of weather, to go out on deck with a hatchet, and literally hack away at the ice, chipping it off. Imagine that duty: climbing the rigging on a tossing and turning boat, in the cold and wet, to cut away sheets of ice. It's a tough job, but a necessary one. So when we talk about vessel stability in this context, it's more complicated, more dangerous, and more difficult than just tipping over a canoe.

CORE THEMES

A key part of putting a case together for litigation, and preparing for trial, is developing your core themes. These are a small number—three to five—of short, clear, strong statements that explain your case and help answer what Juror #6's questions will be about the case. How do you learn what his or her questions will be? By talking to potential jurors. Not in the courtroom but long before: at a bar, at the dinner table, and sitting around with family, friends, and strangers.

Sure, you can talk about your case with other lawyers. But they will not be your jurors. I have long believed that to learn how to present your case, you have to tell the story of the case to nonlawyers, even to complete strangers, and then listen carefully to their questions and reactions. The good news is that most people like to hear stories. Depending on the case, you may need to change names, places, or details to keep it confidential, but it's still interesting. Search for opportunities to tell the story to nonlawyers. The insights you'll get from their questions can be invaluable, and it is from telling the story over and over, and listening to the questions, that you will develop your core themes.

When I told the story of the Gilbert case to friends, family, and strangers, the first core theme that emerged was obvious. "The *Bailey* was a safe and stable vessel." We had to be clear and confident in that belief. But that led to questions, such as "What happened?" and "What went wrong?" Working with our client and our experts, it became clear that the owner had loaded the boat up with oversized equipment. Rather than spend the money to build a bigger boat, he saved money on the size of the boat, but then loaded it up as if it were much bigger. So the second core theme became, "He pretended he had a bigger boat."

Telling the story, though, we realized that was the "what?" but not the "why?" "Why did that matter so much?" "Why did it make it unstable?" Again, going back to our client and experts, we learned the answer, and added the third core theme to the story: "Every pound added above the waterline affects stability." That was the key.

Once you've developed your core themes, the challenge is to present them in a way that the jury will understand and will bring them to life for the jury. Our experts had all kinds of fancy charts and graphics on vessel stability. But the last core theme was so important when I told the story that I felt that before we got to the science, we had to bring it to life. Make it real.

So we did. We got a big aluminum tub, filled it with water, got a toy plastic boat to float in it, and brought the whole thing into the court-room. Then my expert took three metal washers and added them to the top of the boat, one at a time, explaining as he went, roughly as follows:

"Add a little weight above the waterline, and nothing happens."

"Add more weight, and the boat starts to become unstable" (Our little plastic boat started to wobble).

"Add more weight, and over it goes!" (The boat flipped over).

"As you can see, every pound added above the waterline affects stability."

It was an absurdly simple demonstration, but sometimes simple is important. We knew from telling the story to others that our jury had to start with a clear understanding of this concept. From that point on, our experts and other witnesses could talk about stability, and adding weight, with the comfort that they could always refer back to our simple demonstration, and that the jury understood.

"OH CAPTAIN, MY CAPTAIN!"

Vessel stability is a complex science—actually, part science, part art. Stability calculations focus on centers of gravity, centers of buoyancy, the metacenters of vessels, and many other complex calculations. In this case, though, our experts believed that the answer was much simpler. The owner wanted a significantly larger boat but couldn't afford it at the time, so he had Jack design and build this ninety-three-foot boat (still a large fishing vessel!), but then loaded up with heavy gear and extras, as if it was a much larger boat. Like a child decorating a Christmas tree, he put so many heavy ornaments on it that it became top-heavy and unstable. Thus the problem, we believed, was not in the design, but in the owner.

We went to trial in Portland, with the owner claiming the vessel was unstable. Indeed, he had taken the boat down to a shipyard in Louisi-ana and had them essentially cut the boat in half and extend it: make it longer. The theory was that a larger boat would be more stable with all its weight above the waterline. Now he was seeking to recover the cost of that crazy operation, and more, from Jack Gilbert.

Obviously, stability is important with any boat, but with these fishing boats it was particularly so. They go out for days and weeks at a time to the various fishing grounds, including the Grand Banks of Newfoundland. In the years since this trial, the extraordinary weather and seas that fishermen can face out there have been made dramatically clear in movies like *The Perfect Storm* and TV shows like *Deadliest Catch*. We didn't have those reference points at the time so we had to explain to the jury, most of whom were landlubbers, the kinds of extraordinary weather, waves, and winds the boats could be confronted with.

At trial, we had been able to disqualify one of their experts on a Daubert motion, but the court allowed them to substitute in a new expert at the last minute. We objected strongly that this was unfair, but the court overruled our objection. So there we were, Jack Gilbert, myself, and co-counsel, spending the weekend during trial reviewing this new expert's lengthy report. On Saturday night, in the middle of our review, Jack started to laugh. I asked him what could possibly be funny: here we were spending Saturday night desperately trying to figure out how to cross-examine this expert based on his long and highly technical report. But Jack was a wise man, in addition to being a good man. He just stood up with a big smile and said, "You're the lawyer. You're the captain of this trial ship. You have to know this stuff well enough to understand the problem if you're going to cross-examine him. As for me, I'm going out for a beer to celebrate!" And he did.

One of the big issues in vessel stability, not surprisingly, is how weight is distributed around the boat. Our core theme was: every pound added above the waterline affects stability. Think about a sailboat with a deep heavy keel. That's to keep it upright and stable when bending to the wind. Same with a large fishing vessel. The more weight above the waterline, the greater the risk of instability. But how do you measure that? It's a working fishing boat, you can't cut it up and weigh all the pieces, or something crazy like that.

So one thing you have to do is what's called a "weight pick-off." Essentially, you create an inventory of every surface of the boat, determine the measurements for each part of that surface, determine what that surface is made of, determine the weight of that material, and then do the math to figure out how much that piece of the boat weighs.

For example, if one wall of the cabin is made of half-inch-thick steel plating, you have to figure out how many square feet are on that wall, how much a square foot of half-inch steel plating weighs, and then do the math to figure out the weight of that wall.

In this way, slowly, piece by piece, you add everything up to determine what the overall weight is, and where it is. It's an extraordinarily painstaking process. But to be worthwhile, it has to be accurate. Without complete confidence in its accuracy, it's meaningless. It was a long weekend, but somehow, I figured it out, and when Jack came back, he confirmed that, after many long hours, I had found the problem.

Their expert took the stand and gave a pretty nice presentation on direct examination. He had done the weight pick-off, went through it in detail, and determined that the vessel was heavier than it should be above the waterline, and thus potentially unstable. Not dramatically so but enough to cause him concern. Our experts had found no such problems, so now we had a credibility contest.

The "Three Cs" for cross-examination on credibility issues are: Commit, Credit, and Confront. We usually reference these in cross-examining based on a prior inconsistent statement: commit to the current statement, credit the prior statement, and then confront the inconsistency. But the same concepts work for many forms of cross-examination relating to credibility. And so they did here.

> *__Commit:__* I spent time on cross-examination committing him to how important it was to be accurate and precise in doing his weight pick-off. One mistake could throw the whole thing off. I confirmed that he understood boats and navigation, and the purpose of every part of the boat, that he had examined every surface of the vessel carefully to make sure that he was using the correct materials, the correct weights of those materials, and the correct measurements. I confirmed that any errors would call his results into question, and how he had his staff do drawings of each surface, with those measurements, to help explain his work, and he had reviewed those drawings himself to make sure they were accurate. They were all contained in the appendices to his report.

> *__Credit:__* I then spent time using his expertise to credit the functions and navigation of the vessel. Eventually, after some obfuscation

(guilty, Your Honor!), I took a chance, and asked him what was the most important place on the boat? At that point, tired of my apparent ignorance, without hesitation, he said it was the pilot house. Why, I asked (never ask why on cross-examination, unless you bloody well know the answer. Here, I did.). He looked at me with appropriate disdain and explained to this apparent idiot asking the questions that the pilot house was where the captain stood. The captain had to be able to see as much as possible around 360 degrees. It's the key observation point on the boat. I asked for details: It's where the captain steered the boat, observed the crew at work, and kept an eye out for other boats or obstacles? Icebergs? (I couldn't resist.) Yes, of course!

**Confront:** I then asked him if he had done a weight pick-off of the pilot house. Yes, of course, he said, again with some disdain in his voice. Had his staff done drawings to go along with that weight pick-off? Yes. And had he reviewed those drawings? Yes, of course. And did he have the numbers and the drawings from the weight pick-off of the pilot house with him here in trial? Yes, of course. Could you please pull them out for us? So he pulled out the documents for the weight pick-off of the pilot house and placed them in front of him on the witness stand. Very impressive looking.

I had actually thought a good deal about how to take the next step, how to use what I had discovered over the weekend. You should, too, when you have choices like this. There are different approaches, and the decision is often not a simple or easy one. Do I spend time pretending to carefully review the documents and drawings? Do I put them up somewhere for the jury to see? But the disdain in his voice about my apparent lack of understanding of the purpose and importance of the pilot house served to emphasize my point all by itself. So I went right to it.

"Mr. Expert, the walls of the actual pilot house are made of solid steel, correct?

"Yes."

"And the windows of the pilot house are made of clear plexiglass, so the captain has a clean line of sight?"

"Yes."

"Mr. Expert, let me hold up your weight pick-off diagram of the pilot house for the jury and ask you, where is the clear plexiglass?"

After an awkward pause, without waiting for the answer, I asked,

"Mr. Expert, you didn't put any clear plexiglass windows in your weight pick-off of the pilot house? It's all steel?

"Mr. Expert, in fact, you didn't put any windows in the pilot house at all, did you?"

"Mr. Expert, you basically turned the key observation point on the boat into a solid steel bunker that no one could see out of?"

"Mr. Expert, clear plexiglass for the windows weighs a lot less than the half-inch solid steel you put in there, doesn't it?"

This went on for a little while. The case was never appealed (we won!), so there is no trial transcript. And this is all from memory. Forgive me if it's not exact, but you get the idea. In fact, the difference in weight between clear plexiglass and solid steel, though significant, probably did not completely negate his weight pick-off. But his "expert" "precise" "of course" design of the pilot house, as a solid steel bunker, certainly did. Almost instantly, he lost all credibility with the jury. He was pretty much useless as an expert.

Yes, this was a last-minute replacement expert witness. Yes, he necessarily had to do an extraordinary amount of work very quickly. Yes, counsel had not had as much time as they might have liked to review his work with him. But as trial lawyers, we are the captain of the ship. The case is our responsibility, not the experts. We have to know the territory! One of the many lessons I learned from Jack Gilbert during this great trial was from his laughter walking out of the room that Saturday night going for a beer. He was not going to spoon-feed me when I had to learn it myself. He was not going to allow me to essentially cede control of the case to him by relying entirely on him to find the obvious flaw in the other side's expert report. He understood that is not the way to captain the ship, any more than trying to do so from inside a solid steel bunker. Lessons learned.

10

SG Limited

EXECUTIVE SUMMARY

Defense of a civil case brought by the Securities and Exchange Commission (SEC) against an Internet fantasy stock game.

As you read this chapter, be aware of:

- **Storytelling**: The facts and the law are important, but juries, like all of us, need to know the story, and respond best when the story is a compelling one.

- **Pyrrhic victories/successful losses**: Our goal as trial lawyers is not just to win one round but to win the whole match. Sometimes the lesser win can lead to a greater loss.

- **In a good settlement, everyone gives a little**: Sometimes in a settlement negotiation, you can get what you want, but still let the other side save a little face.

INTRODUCTION

In the late 1990s, as the internet became more widely accessible and useable, a wave of new internet games developed, attracting game developers and players from all over the world. Suddenly, it didn't matter much where the game was created or where the players were located. Online knew few barriers and was growing fast.

In this environment, a couple of computer geeks in Hungary and several places around the globe got together and developed an internet stock game. The idea was that they made up several fantasy companies with fun names and descriptions. Players would pay money to join the game and pick their companies. Then the price of the stocks would go up and down randomly, based, as best I could tell, on what the game's organizers had for breakfast or other whims. No real rhyme or reason for any of it.

Silly? Yes, it was—and absurdly simple and pedestrian compared to today's highly sophisticated computer games. But their timing caught the wave of new internet games, and it took off. Players from around the world found it to be something new and fun. Although none of the organizers were from the United States (and some of the English in the game's website and instructions were clearly not from native English speakers), the largest number of players ended up being Americans.

Everyone was having fun. The reviews on the game from players were great, and the number of players grew exponentially—largely by word of mouth. It cost some money to play, but no one was losing big bucks, and presumably everyone understood that it was just a game. As the website for this "virtual game" made clear (even if the English was not), "Player's entering the website is solely for Player's own personal entertainment . . ."

Alas, the Securities and Exchange Commission (SEC) was neither entertained nor amused. Regulators rarely have a sense of humor. They filed a civil complaint against the game company, SG Limited, in federal court under the US securities laws, including an *ex parte* motion (one party—without giving SG notice) to freeze SG's bank accounts. In so doing, they froze (or "infrigidated," as the First Circuit Court of Appeals would later describe it—great word) about $5,500,000.

Without getting too far into the weeds, the SEC had two basic claims. First, that the "shares" of these virtual companies were, in fact, securities; SG had failed to register these securities with the SEC, and thus they had violated the law. Second, that this was a "Ponzi scheme," essentially robbing Peter to pay Paul. As the Court of Appeals explained, Ponzi schemes are "named after the notorious Boston swindler Charles Ponzi, who parlayed an initial stake of $150 into a fortune by means of an elaborate scheme featuring promissory notes yielding interest at annual rates of up to 50%—money tendered by later investors . . . used to pay off earlier investors."[1]

STORYTELLING

At the time, I had a small law firm in Boston with two friends—Butters, Brazilian, and Small. SG came to me to defend them in the SEC's suit, and I went into court with a motion to dismiss the case and unfreeze the money. In our memorandum in support of the motion, and our lengthy oral argument before Judge Tauro, I essentially argued that while the SEC might not have a sense of humor, the law did—or it should. This was unquestionably just a game with make-believe stocks and willing players. These were not legal securities, and the players were not being fooled or defrauded by a fantasy game.

As trial lawyers, we wear many hats: advocates, teachers, dealmakers, writers, preachers, and more. But first and foremost, we are storytellers. Taking the law and the evidence, and weaving together the story that helps the jury to understand and relate to our case. To be effective, we cannot just recite the facts; we have to tell a story to help the jury feel what happened, not just learn it. For many years, I have had a wonderful Native American proverb on my wall:

> "Tell me the facts and I'll learn,
> Tell me the truth and I'll believe.
> But tell me a story, and
> It will live in my heart forever."

That should be the mantra for anyone wanting to try cases: find the story of your case and develop the best way to tell it.

SG Limited is one of my favorite examples. It was a technical securities issue that actually was a great story. A couple of computer geeks from around the world, sitting at their keyboards, connecting with each other and making up a funny fantasy that people loved to play. The fun, and the game, were clear throughout, including from the "companies" themselves. The one I loved best was the "fart company", whose purpose was to harness and sell methane gas from—you guessed it—human

---

[1] Securities & Exchange Commission v. SG Ltd., 265 F3d 42, footnote 3 (1st Cir. 2001).

flatulence. Ridiculous? Of course it was, that was part of the fun and part of the story.

That was the key point. The essence of a security had to be a basis in reality. the essence of a "Ponzi scheme" was the fraud, not just the source of the funds. If "robbing Peter to pay Paul" by itself was against the law, even if both Peter and Paul understood it was just a game, I argued, Las Vegas would have to shut down tomorrow. After all, following the SEC's argument, what is a casino but a giant, nonstop "Ponzi scheme" without the fraud. The casino can only pay me my winnings at the tables because someone else—actually lots of someone elses—is losing.

I walked the court through the language of the game's website, freely admitting that the English was not perfect, but that the message was clear. Ultimately, the story was more persuasive than the technical legal argument. Looking at the website, Judge Tauro found, "It is difficult to imagine more clear and forceful language alerting potential participants that they would be playing a game, not making an investment."[2] On that basis, the court found that these were not securities under the law, nor was it an illegal "Ponzi scheme." The District Court granted our motion to dismiss the SEC's case. The story had won the day.

PYRRHIC VICTORIES/SUCCESSFUL LOSSES

Undaunted, the SEC appealed the dismissal to the First Circuit Court of Appeals. We filed extensive briefs and had another lengthy oral argument, going back and forth between our story and the SEC's view of the law. But as often happens at the appellate level, the narrow law wins over the broader story. In a 14-page opinion, the Court of Appeals reversed the District Court's dismissal. It did an extensive technical analysis of the law and came to the conclusion that there was enough in the SEC's complaint to get it a past a motion to dismiss. The first time I read through the opinion, I was devastated. The SEC had won.

But had they? Yes, at that early stage, on a motion to dismiss, but in the long run? The second time I read through the opinion, the power

---

[2] Ibid., F. Supp 126, 130.

of the story started to come through. The court repeatedly emphasized that this was only a motion to dismiss. At that early stage, the court reviews the case, "accepting as true all well-pleaded factual arguments and indulging all reasonable influences in the plaintiff's favor." If there are factual disputes, if there is a broader story, that is for another day. "It is not this Court's place to resolve such fact-sensitive questions in the context of a . . . motion for dismissal."[3]

To the SEC's dismay, though, it was clear that even the legalistic Court of Appeals had heard and understood the story. Throughout the opinion were several statements by the court indicating trouble ahead for the SEC at trial. Parts of our story that, "give(s) rise to an issue of fact (or perhaps multiple issues of fact)."[4] In an extraordinary shot across the bow to the SEC, near the end of its opinion, the Court stated:

> This is not to say that SG's gaming language and repeated disclaimers are irrelevant. SG has a plausible argument, forcefully advanced by able counsel, that no participant in his or her right mind should have expected guaranteed profits from purchases of privileged company shares.[5]

Even though the SEC had "won" that round in the Court of Appeals, it was at least partially a pyrrhic victory, if it signaled a possible loss at trial. So, not surprisingly, the SEC approached us about a settlement. I was happy to tell the SEC that "able counsel" was looking forward to "forcefully advancing" this "plausible argument" at trial. We had a story to tell, and witnesses who could tell it.

What was their story, I asked them? It was one thing to win a technical legal argument at the Court of Appeals, but trials were about stories. What was their story? And just as important, for evaluating any story for trial, who would tell it? Who would come into a federal court, raise their right hand, take the oath, and swear to the jury that they thought that the "fart company" was real, or that this self-described "virtual game" was not just a game.

---

[3] Securities & Exchange Commission v. SG Ltd., 265 F.3d 42 (1st Cir. 2001).

[4] *Id.*

[5] *Id.*

IN A GOOD SETTLEMENT, EVERYONE GIVES A LITTLE

Our client was happy to settle. The game had been fun, but it had run its course. They were willing to move on to the next adventure. But they wanted their money back, the $5,500,000 that the SEC had frozen. No, we were told, the SEC never does that. Several lawyers I spoke with who were much more familiar with the SEC than I was, confirmed it: they had never heard of the SEC giving back money that they had seized.

But my clients were adamant: give us back the money you took, or we go to trial. We pushed hard on the story, and how bad the SEC would look, pushing such a technical case against a virtual game. "Call your first witness!" I said, which is what I've always said to anyone—either as a prosecutor or in private practice—who comes into my office with a far-fetched case. Who would that be? Who would testify that this was real? Who could testify on direct without then giving us the opportunity to tell our story on cross-examination? Do you want to give us our money back now, or risk having to give it back after an embarrassing loss at trial?

Once again, the story came to our rescue. We believed the players all understood this was just a game. So I relied on that belief. I proposed a face-saving compromise for the SEC: Give us back most of the money, and we'll agree that the remainder be set aside in a separate fund. If any player submits a signed, sworn affidavit within a set period of time (I think it was six months) that they believed these stocks were real (including of course, the "fart company") and profits were truly guaranteed, they could get their money back out of the fund. It was a way for the SEC to save face, to show that they were protecting the "victims," while at the same time for us highlighting the absurdity of their case.

We believed our story. We believed that no one would come forward to sign such an affidavit and submit it to the SEC, admitting to such foolishness. And we were right. No one ever did. The client got back their money, even though the SEC supposedly never gives back money. The case went away, without any finding or admission of wrongdoing, even though the SEC had won in the Court of Appeals, and the client was happy with our story and with the result.

In any case, we should not just focus on the bits and pieces of law and evidence. Find the story that binds them together and focus on that. At every stage of the case. That's the lesson of SG.

11

Gov. Edwin Edwards

EXECUTIVE SUMMARY

Defense of former Louisiana Gov. Edwin Edwards on charges of illegally accepting money to assist in riverboat gambling licenses.
  As you read this chapter, be aware of:

- **Cases come in many ways:** Be ready and be flexible; cases come in the door from many directions.

- **"Nature abhors a vacuum"**—So does the media: recognize that the media and the court of public opinions are important aspects of many high-profile cases.

- **"A fair and impartial judge":** The courtroom environment and players are often not ideal. We cannot lose faith and have to keep pushing forward.

- **All eyes on the client**: We represent our clients in court but we also have to recognize that what goes on outside of court can impact them, and thus our cases.

- **Adapting to the courtroom**: Jurors can spot a phony: you have to be yourself and adapt as best you can to the environment around you.

GOV. EDWIN EDWARDS

I have been fortunate enough since I went into private practice to represent some extraordinary, high-profile clients over the years. Alas, some of them don't lend themselves to this kind of discussion because of issues of attorney-client privilege, and other reasons. Perhaps the one to linger on is Edwin Edwards, an extraordinary figure in Louisiana—and national politics. He first ran for office in 1954 (Crowley City Council) at the age of twenty-seven, and last ran for office in 2014 (US Congress) at age eighty-seven. During those sixty years in public life, his positions included four terms as a congressman and four four-year terms as governor. In the tradition of the late great Huey Long, for many years he *was* Louisiana politics.

His political legacy included many good things, including spending on human services and education, and bringing greater diversity to all levels of state government.

His intellectual legacy was as a great debater (early in life he wanted to be a preacher, and later became a trial lawyer), and the master of the one-line zinger. He could—and did—unshakingly define his opponents by his quick one-liners. For example:

Of one opponent's intellect: He's "so slow that it takes him ninety minutes to watch Sixty Minutes."[1]

In a debate, where his opponent asked rhetorically, "How come you talk out of both sides of your mouth?", Edwards shot back: "So people like you with only half a brain can understand."[2]

In his race against former KKK Grand Wizard David Duke, Edwards referred to his considerable reputation as a ladies' man, saying, "The only place where David Duke and I are alike is we are both wizards under the sheets."[3]

His personal legacy was more mixed. Although he was widely loved by many in Louisiana, he also cherished his image as a loveable rogue, and teased or crossed the ethical lines. He was dogged by various

---

[1] *The Advocate*, November 1, 2009.

[2] Louisiana Public Broadcasting, *Campaign 1983: The Treen/Edwards Debates, No. 2*, YouTube (July 14, 2021), https://www.youtube.com/watch?v=hPlLri8NFqs.

[3] *The Advocate*, July 12, 2021.

scandals and investigations. Finally, in 1998, he was indicted on federal racketeering and corruption charges, alleging that he illegally took money to help people get state riverboat gambling licenses. The government had wiretap recordings of both Edwin and his son, Steven, also a lawyer and a co-defendant.

CASES COME IN MANY WAYS

Although Edwin had a well-known local criminal lawyer representing him, it was clear the case would be difficult and complex, with several challenging federal law issues, including the wiretaps, the Racketeer Influenced and Corrupt Organizations Act (RICO), and more.

Edwin realized that they needed some broader federal experience on the team, so they reached out to Jim Cole in Washington, DC. Jim was—and is—a great friend and a great lawyer, although the difficulties of this case strained our friendship for a while. We met when we both started at the Department of Justice in Washington, DC. We shared a love of music, a sense of humor, an office for a while, and a sailboat, on which we took many adventures. He had prosecuted significant cases in Louisiana before he left DOJ for private practice, so he knew the territory and was known.

Jim came in to represent Steven, so Edwin still had the Louisiana counsel. But as Jim worked with the team in Louisiana, he eventually came to the conclusion that they needed more federal case/big case help, and he recommended they consider me. At the time, I was practicing in Boston. A lawyer whom I had known and liked since we were on opposite sides when I was in the US Attorney's Office, Tom Butters and I, together with a friend of Tom's, John Brazilian, had founded our own firm, Butters, Brazilian and Small (as you can imagine, with two adjectives and a verb as names, it took some work to get the proper sequence). We eventually had eight to ten lawyers, and it was a fun way to practice.

My memory may be off a bit on the months, but not by much. As I recall, Edwin's case was set for trial in January in federal court in Baton Rouge: a long way from Boston in many respects. So, despite some warning from Jim, it was still a surprise when my office phone rang in October, just three months before trial, and it was Edwin Edwards, asking if I would come down to Louisiana and take over as his counsel.

After some haggling over money and terms—imagine haggling with a world-class haggler—I agreed and headed south.

"NATURE ABHORS A VACUUM"—SO DOES THE MEDIA

The first of many shocks was just the news of my hiring. I had been involved in various high-profile cases before, but none where my involvement was itself a big story. This was different. Edwin Edwards, a Louisiana legend, replaced his renowned local attorney with someone from . . . where? Boston? You might as well have said Timbuktu down on the Bayou. Why had he done such a thing? There had to be a secret reason. So the speculation ran rampant in the media, with the idea building that I had somehow been hired to cut a deal. We had no interest in getting into the middle of that maelstrom, but with no statement from us, the rumor just fed on itself.

In any high-profile case, it's often a difficult decision when to speak and when to remain silent. Aristotle said, "Nature abhors a vacuum."[4] He was talking about physics, not the media, but the same rule applies. Without contravention, the rumor built on itself exponentially, until Louisiana's biggest TV station ran a lengthy lead report about how I had been hired to go around the local US Attorney and cut a deal for Edwin with my good friend, then US Attorney General Janet Reno. With lots of fanfare and purported details.

None of it was true, of course. I'd been hired to try the case. And although I have great respect for Janet Reno, we actually had never met at the time—much less as good friends. There was no discussion with anyone of a guilty plea. But in Louisiana, politics and sports are both big stories: politics as sport, and sports as politics. So no surprise, I guess, that the two biggest stories for a week or two were Edwin hiring me and LSU firing their football coach. The two stories took turns being in the lead.

The day after the lead story was on TV, we happened to have a motion hearing before the judge. I cannot remember what the motions were, but it was the first time that I would appear in public as Edwin's lawyer, so there was a huge crowd of reporters and cameras waiting on the courthouse steps when the hearing ended. With multiple defendants, lawyers, families, friends, and hangers-on, we always moved with a

---

[4] Aristotle, *Physics* (350 BC).

big crowd of people. As we walked toward the front doors of the court-house, Edwin saw the media mob and calmly motioned for everyone to stop, which of course they did. Then he casually took my arm, and with me just following his lead, we sauntered out onto the front steps.

Once we were out on the steps, it was chaos. The media mob was shouting questions at both of us: was there a deal, would we plead guilty, why was I there? Partially, they wanted to get answers to confirm the rumors they had been touting. Partially, they wanted me to speak so they could film me speaking in tongues, or however creatures from Boston (or Timbuktu) spoke. Instead, Edwin held up his hands for quiet and solemnly said that he had an important announcement to make. Shocked silence from the crowd. This is what they'd been telling their audience; it was the announcement of a deal. Edwin Edwards, the ultimate fighter, was going to plead guilty.

And Edwin, of course, was the master of the moment. After a brief pause, he went on: "I've thought about this deeply, I've prayed about it, I've discussed it at length with my family." Long pause. Here it comes. The mob held its breath. "And after deep contemplation, I've decided to turn down the job of LSU football coach, if it's offered!" A heartbeat of confused silence, then a burst of appreciative laughter. The master of the one-liner had done it again, this time to the very reporters who had reveled in his past zingers. Edwin waved thank-you, and the two of us sauntered off. And that was it. The rumors stopped. The story ends here. Everyone in the media understood that they had been schooled: called to task for following false leads and generating false rumors. Get a life.

Of course, the media often gets the last laugh, and they got it here on me through a one-liner of their own. During trials, I often try to get outside briefly during the afternoon break. It lets you stretch your legs, get some fresh air, and take a minute. During the long Edwards trial, I would try every day to go out to the little park next to the courthouse, where I would sit on a bench and drink a Barq's root beer. The media mob was restricted to an area by the courthouse steps, some distance away. At first, they would wave and try to shout questions, but eventually gave up when I just waved back, and they respected my little break. One day, though, I was sick with the flu, so when I came out and sat on the bench, I put my head back and closed my eyes, just for a couple of minutes. One of the news photographers across the park had a long-range lens and took a picture. The next day on the front page of the newspaper was that picture with the caption: "The Defense Rests."

"A FAIR AND IMPARTIAL JUDGE"

Trials are human events and thus, like the humans who conduct them, are imperfect. As trial lawyers, part of our mission is to search out those imperfections and deal with them as best as we can: whether in jury selection, choosing and preparing our witnesses, cross-examining the other side's witnesses, and more. Judicial imperfections, though, can be more difficult to address, and sometimes impossible.

Litigants in any case rely on a fair and impartial judge to preside over a trial. The jury, of course, decides the ultimate verdict, but the trial judge makes a multitude of rulings, large and small, that can impact the case, and what is presented to the jury for their consideration. In any jurisdiction, there can be judges who are considered "pro-government" or "pro-defense." Sometimes it's based on their background—a former prosecutor or former defense counsel. Sometimes it's political or philosophical. But it's usually not personal.

Most jurisdictions, particularly for federal courts, are large enough that the judge is unlikely to have any knowledge of, or history with, the defendant. And most defendants are just not that widely known. Not so in Louisiana. The state itself is small: its total population is smaller than Greater Boston. And politics and government are even smaller worlds. Edwin Edwards had been a dominant figure in Louisiana politics for four decades, so few people in politics and government didn't know him. And to know him was generally to love him or hate him: few people were neutral about Edwards.

So, if someone worked their way up the ladder in politics and government, to become—let's say—a federal judge, it's likely that they had a history with Edwin. Good or bad. The judge in our case had a long history, and it was a bad one. Edwin supposedly had passed him over for a position he coveted many years before, and the judge had hated Edwin ever since. If the incident had been more recent and documented, we might have been able to have the judge removed. But it was long ago in time—though not in memory—and not documented. So we were stuck with a judge who apparently had a long-standing hatred of our client.

And he was so pleasant about it. He would smile and say nice things about us, as he pulled our legs out from under us and cut us to ribbons. Every day. Nearly every day, for almost three months, Jim and I would walk to court and ask each other, "How is he going to screw us today?"

It was a hell of a way to have to start each trial day. I'm not sure that I ever fully appreciated the ancient form of Chinese torture called Ling-chi, also known as "Death by a Thousand Cuts."

But this was it. Every day, more cuts.

What could we do? Try our case. Be as prepared, zealous, and determined as possible. Keep pushing. Understand that it was not a level playing field, and buckle up and keep playing anyway. Not to say it was easy, it was not. It was difficult, stressful, and exhausting. And we had the added burden of trying to keep our client's spirits up, as well. But that's what's required. Do the best you can for your client, regardless of the circumstances.

ALL EYES ON THE CLIENT

Trials are stressful for lawyers. But don't lose sight of how much more stressful it may be for the client. In a new and strange environment, their liberty, money, family, reputation, and more may be at stake. Meanwhile, while all eyes are upon them, they have to keep themselves carefully under control. They cannot lash out at those who lie about them, shake their head in anger when the judge rules against them, or do any of the things normal people would do in such an abnormal situation. Instead, they have to look pleasantly and passively at who may be determining the rest of their lives, and quietly put their fate in the hands of a relative stranger: you, their lawyer.

Edwin Edwards was not an easy client. He had spent much of his life in positions of power, being in control. Plus, he had been a trial lawyer at one point, so he felt like he knew his way around the courtroom. With that background, ceding control of the courtroom and the trial to this stranger from Boston was tough. We argued, we fired each other a couple of times. One time I was literally in my little temporary apartment packing to go home, and he sent his son Steven over to make peace.

But we had a case to try, and I needed him working closely with us and in good spirits. In any case, that means being aware of the client's needs and doing our best to accommodate them, including maintaining some sense of normalcy despite the chaos and pressure. In Louisiana, not surprisingly, that meant food. Leading up to the trial, lots of friends reached out and wanted to do something to help the governor. We realized that one thing they could do was cook.

Our great paralegal in Baton Rogue had a house just a couple blocks from the courthouse that became our headquarters. With multiple defendants, lawyers, family, friends, and hangers-on, everywhere we went there was a crowd. Lunch posed a challenge. So we set up a schedule of volunteers to cook lunch every day at our paralegal's house. The court would break for lunch, and this whole crowd would walk over to the house to eat.

And what a lunch it was. Imagine being in Louisiana, where food is such a part of their pride, life, and culture, and being invited to cook lunch for the governor. We're not talking about peanut butter and jelly sandwiches. Every day was a surprise: barbeque pits set up in the driveway, big pots of creole on the stove, you name it. Edwin would want us to sit down and eat with him, even if it was a working lunch, which it usually was. And then back to court after that big (delicious) lunch, and feeling stuffed and groggy by midafternoon.

And then there was dinner. We were fighting a long, difficult trial, with the deck stacked against us. Worse still, one of the things the judge did was rule that the prosecution did not have to tell us what witnesses they were going to call each day until the end of the day before. So each day at about 5 p.m., the prosecution would give us their witness list for the next day. Often they stacked the list with people they had no intention of calling, just to throw us off. So each day, after a long trial day, we would begin a second "day" of researching and preparing for the witnesses.

So who had time for dinner? In most trials, if you could grab a quick bite, you were lucky. But this was Louisiana, and this was the governor. Dinner was an important part of life, and he often insisted that we sit down and join him. So we did. And it helped our client—and all of us— maintain a sense of normalcy. In most trials, if anything, I lose weight from working hard and not eating. In Louisiana, we made time for our client. All of these years later, I still carry around some of the excess weight I gained in those months in Louisiana.

On occasion, maintaining normalcy went beyond food. One evening, the governor invited me to come with him to a big charity event, a boxing match. When I asked for more details, he explained that it was between boxing teams of local firefighters on the one hand and local police on the other. The event was humorously named, "Guns and Hoses." I was not amused. "Edwin, we have work to do. Plus, we're in the middle of one of the biggest criminal trials in Louisiana history. I'm not sure it's a good idea to go parade in front of thousands of police officers and firefighters." You don't get it, he replied, these are my people.

He was right, of course. Edwin was one of the last of the true progressive populists, appealing to several constituencies. We entered the auditorium to great cheers and were shown to ringside seats. Throughout the matches, a steady stream of people came up to wish him well— "Give 'em hell, Governor!" was a common refrain. At one point, the ring announcer pointed him out to the crowd and welcomed "The greatest Governor this great state has ever had!" to the roar of the crowd. It was quite a night and reenergized our client.

We were representing a client in trial. But often we have to help the client outside of the courtroom, to give them the ability to survive and thrive in the courtroom.

ADAPTING TO THE COURTROOM

I was never going to be the local boy who made good in this trial. Telling heartwarming stories of growing up on the Bayou. So, what to do? Use what you have. Take advantage of who you are. During the three-month trial, there were innumerable difficult Cajun words: names, places, etc. It fairly quickly became a game of sorts with the jury: that I would predictably botch the pronunciation, and we would laugh about it together. A shared joke.

When wealthy Eddie DeBartolo, the owner of the San Francisco 49ers NFL team, testified to paying the former governor $400,000 to get a riverboat gambling license, I tried to use our common distance from his wealth to ridicule the idea that he was somehow threatened or intimidated by Edwin. I argued that he was the one who reached out, and that given his extraordinary wealth, $400,000 was no big deal to him.

Finally, in closing argument, I acknowledged the obvious, that I was "not from here," and tried to use my own background to help the jury relate. I talked about growing up in Lexington, Massachusetts, site of the first shots of the American Revolution. I recited my favorite quote from that battle, Captain John Parker exalting his ragtag group of farmers and merchants to "Stand by your ground, don't fire unless fired upon, but if they mean to have a war, let it begin here." Stand your ground, I said, against government overreaching, against trial by rumor or innuendo. It was a rousing speech.

In the end, it didn't work. A combination of Edwin's reputation, the government's wiretaps and the judge's bulldozing overwhelmed us. The jury found Edwin guilty on enough of the counts to send him to jail. But it was a fascinating case, about a fascinating character, with many lessons learned.

12

Panitz

EXECUTIVE SUMMARY

Defense of the "Jerry Springer Murder" defendant, in Sarasota, Florida.

As you read this chapter, be aware of:

- **"Be ready when the bell rings"**: Cases arise in many ways and at all hours. Be ready to respond.

- **Know your limits:** The law is a specialized profession—by subject matter, by jurisdiction, and in other ways. Know your limits and get the help you need to properly represent your client.

- **Negotiations happen in different ways:** Negotiations can begin in different ways and take unexpected turns along the way.

PANITZ

Ralf Panitz was a forty-year-old part-time house painter, a German citizen, but had lived near Sarasota, Florida, for some years. He had divorced his wife, Nancy, and now lived with his new wife, Eleanor. But Nancy still lived in their marital home and still dreamed of reuniting with her ex-husband, although Ralf and Eleanor tried to tell her it was over. A rather ordinary story of rather ordinary people. It turned out later that it was far more complicated and uglier, but that's how it appeared at the time.

Somehow, this ordinary tale got into the hands of the Jerry Springer Show. Springer was a pioneer of trash TV and hosted a controversial but popular show from 1991 to 2018. The show thrived on creating controversy, fights, and more. Typical of the show, they apparently lied to both sides to convince them to come on. Ex-wife Nancy believed that she was coming on to reunite with Ralf. Meanwhile, Ralf and Eleanor believed that here was their chance to convince Nancy that it was over.

The show's schedule promised: "Eleanor says her husband's ex-wife, Nan, won't take no for an answer. Nan stalked them so severely that they had to go into hiding. Today, Nan will learn that her ex-husband is actually married to Eleanor!" It was a twisted version of the truth, but the truth came second to the drama.

Why anyone would agree to go on national TV to try to resolve their personal problems this way is beyond me. But it was what the Jerry Springer show fed on. So, the three of them were separately flown up to Chicago, put up in a nice hotel, escorted into the studio, and went on camera—with predictable results. When they learned that it was all a lie, rather than get mad at the con man who had put them in this position, they got mad at each other, and a screaming fight ensued, just as the Springer folks had hoped for. Great TV.

So, they all went home disappointed. Unfortunately, shortly thereafter, ex-wife Nancy was found dead in the former marital home. The "Jerry Springer Murder," as it was called, was a huge story. There were no eyewitnesses, and not much basis to link Ralf to the crime—after all, he was happily married and living elsewhere. He had not been charged with anything, but he was certainly high on the suspect list. Nevertheless, Ralf and Eleanor apparently decided that this would be a good time to leave Sarasota for a bit and see the country. So, they got into their Subaru and left town.

According to the press, they were headed for Canada, but apparently, they got as far as Boston and then ran out of money. Not sure what else to do, Panitz decided to take advantage of his German citizenship, and they showed up at the German Consulate in Boston, looking for help. Some of the press later reported, as *The Guardian* said, that "police tracked Ralf and Eleanor down to Boston . . . [and] after being captured, Ralf was brought back to Florida . . ." But that's not at all what really happened.

BE READY WHEN THE BELL RINGS

Ralf's showing up unannounced threw the German Consulate into a bit of a panic. He had not yet been indicted, but he was a high-profile suspect in a high-profile murder case. Like most consulates, they dealt mostly with commercial and visa issues. Panitz brought visions of police Special Weapons and Tactics (SWAT) teams, and TV news cameras, surrounding the consulate, in search of a murder suspect. So, they called a lawyer. But the U.S. lawyers they dealt with were, of course, largely for commercial and visa issues, not criminal law. The corporate lawyer they called didn't know what to do either, so she picked up the phone and called her former partner—me.

Have you ever been just about to leave somewhere—home, office, wherever—when the phone rings, and you can't decide whether to pick it up or let the voicemail handle it until tomorrow? It was 5:30 p.m. The staff was gone. I was leaving the office, heading to meet a friend for a drink. And the phone rang. What to do? But as a friend of mine says about the work we do, "If they didn't have fires, they wouldn't need firefighters!" So I answered the phone. The next thing I knew, I was grabbing an associate who was still in the office and heading to the German Consulate.

At the consulate, I first met with the consular staff and tried to ease their fears. Then I met with Ralf and Eleanor and started to interview them. Before I got very far, the consul came into the conference room in an agitated state. A story had just come over the news wires: Ralf had been indicted in Florida for first-degree murder, and there was a warrant issued for his arrest. Then came the next surprise of the night: Florida is a capital punishment state. As a defendant charged with first-degree murder, Ralf was facing the death penalty.

Germany's national policies are strongly opposed to the death penalty. I don't know the history behind it, but it's their clear policy today. And the spectacle of a German citizen being sentenced to death by an American court did not sit well: diplomatically, politically, or morally. It was quickly clear that Ralf could not afford private defense counsel. Germany generally does not interfere with the American justice system, and is content with its citizens utilizing public defenders, if necessary. But not when it's life or death and a potential diplomatic nightmare. So, the consul consulted with his superiors back home, and then informed me that the German government would pay my fees to represent Ralf.

KNOW YOUR LIMITS

I very quickly did several things.

First, I called a great criminal defense lawyer I knew in Miami who had handled murder cases, Jayne Weintraub, and asked her to join the team. Fortunately, she said yes. Everyone knows that medicine is specialized. You don't go to a knee doctor for a problem with your eyes. But most lay people don't realize how specialized the law is, and too many lawyers don't tell them. The reality is that most lawyers are not litigators, most litigators rarely if ever go to trial, most trial lawyers don't do criminal defense, and most criminal defense lawyers have never handled murder cases. I was licensed in Florida and an experienced criminal trial lawyer, but for a capital murder case in Florida, under Florida criminal law, and state court rules and procedures, I needed local murder expertise. Jayne was it. And she quickly brought in a great private investigator that she worked with. We agreed to meet the next morning at the Tampa Airport.

Next, I called the Sarasota County District Attorney's Office. I was able to get through to an assistant district attorney covering off-hour emergencies. I introduced myself, told her I was in Boston and had just been retained by Ralf (I didn't tell her who was paying—and she didn't ask), we had just learned about the indictment, and we would travel to Florida first thing in the morning to voluntarily surrender him. Would they please withdraw the arrest warrant, so there would not be any incident as we traveled to meet them. She refused. She said she didn't know me, didn't know if I was telling the truth, and would not do anything to lift the warrant. I told her we would be at her office at noon the next day.

Next, I called the airline to get us plane tickets to Tampa early in the morning (This was before 9/11 and all the heightened security. With an outstanding arrest warrant, today we would probably have never made it onto the plane). And I called the Lenox Hotel, across from my office, to book us all rooms for the night. We spoke briefly with Ralf in the rooms, and then all went to bed, exhausted.

When we landed in Tampa the next morning, Jayne met us at the airport, and we rented a van for the drive to Sarasota. Time was precious now, and we needed the van as a moving conference room to meet privately with our client. I gave the keys to my associate and warned him: stay under the speed limit and don't do anything stupid. I don't want us to get pulled over. Imagine a highway patrol officer somehow recognizing Ralf, and a whole incident happening, or worse. Probably made him even more nervous than he was before, but we had to be smart about this.

Although the assistant district attorney had said she didn't know me enough to rely on me, apparently that was not entirely true. When we arrived at the Sarasota County Courthouse at noon, as promised, there was a full gaggle of reporters, TV cameras, and others waiting to meet us. We certainly hadn't called the media from the plane. Clearly, the assistant district attorney had trusted my promise of bringing Ralf in around noon enough that she had made sure that the press was there to make a splash.

Once we finished the "perp walk" past the cameras and into the courthouse, Ralf was processed and then set for a bail hearing. Given the seriousness of the offense, Ralf's lack of roots in the community, and the fact that he was already once most of the way to Canada (although he did come back voluntarily, we argued), it was no surprise that bail was denied. With that part of the drama over, it was time to turn to his defense.

That's when having a local expert was really important. Most people are at least vaguely familiar with discovery in a civil lawsuit: written interrogatories, requests for documents, depositions, and much more. The irony is that although there is often so much more at stake in a criminal trial—life, liberty, reputation, etc.—in federal court and most state jurisdictions, there is far less discovery allowed to the defense. Fortunately, Jayne gave me a detailed lesson on how different the law was in Florida, where the defense is allowed extensive discovery. I was pleasantly surprised.

NEGOTIATIONS HAPPEN IN DIFFERENT WAYS

So we mapped out and started implementing an extensive discovery plan. Written discovery, document requests, deposition subpoenas, interviews by our private investigator, and more. The district attorney's office was taken by surprise. Their evidence at the outset was thin, but they assumed that they would have time to develop their case without interference. After all, the defendant was a part-time painter, without any assets to pay for lawyers and investigators, and a German citizen without any real familiarity with the system. How was all of this happening? How had we appeared on the scene? Who was paying for it all? It was a mystery to them.

Like any negotiations, guilty plea-deal negotiations can start in different ways. Sometimes one party picks up the phone, sometimes a casual chat in the courthouse hallway, sometimes one party makes a move with the clear but unspoken message: your turn. That's what happened here. After about two weeks (as I recall) of being bombarded by our discovery and investigation, the district attorney's office, without telling us in advance, lowered the charges from first-degree to second-degree murder, thus taking the death penalty off the table. Clearly, it was an opening move, and our turn to respond with a proposal.

But negotiations can be highly unpredictable. The district attorney's office didn't know who was paying our bills or why. Therefore, they didn't know what the more immediate effect of their move would be. When I called the German Consulate to report this great victory, they were thrilled. But their next reaction was to say: congratulations, many thanks, send us your bill, you're done! With the death penalty off the table, the German government was no longer willing to fund the defense. Period. Jayne and I tried to figure out a way that we could stay on, but it just wasn't feasible.

So we reluctantly had to withdraw from the case. Ralf's case went downhill from there. More evidence was uncovered against him, he changed lawyers at least once or twice, and eventually he was convicted. But before all that happened, when we announced our withdrawal, the headline in the Sarasota newspaper was, "Attorney Dream Team Drops Panitz." I've always wanted to be the leader of a "dream team," and for a short while, there we were.

13

Reflections:
State v. Faulkner

═══════════ EXECUTIVE SUMMARY ═══════════

Double murder prosecution against defendant Ashley Faulkner.
Reflecting back on lessons learned, including:

1. Law as a force for change;

2. Core themes/ storytelling;

3. Juror #6;

4. Finding common ground with the judge;

5. "Bring Out the Bad Stuff" (BOBS);

6. Cross-examination.

INTRODUCTION

Ashley Faulkner was charged with the murder of Bo Wozniak and
Savanah Hyde. Wozniak was found shot in his bed in his apartment.
His girlfriend, Hyde, was found in the apartment bathroom, shot in
the head, with the gun next to her. At first, it looked like a murder-
suicide, but that soon changed. Ashley Faulkner was a security guard at

the apartment complex. Shaun Royce, one of the other guards, testified to the grand jury that he saw Faulkner on the night of the murder coming out of Wozniak's apartment. Faulkner wanted to date Hyde and was jealous of Wozniak.

Another witness, Casey Lauper, was the registered owner of the gun found in the bathroom that was used to shoot Wozniak and Hyde. Lauper testified that Faulkner, who he knew, tried to buy the gun from him. After he showed Falkner the gun in his locker, it went missing.

Lauper's roommate, Jan Butler, was a former girlfriend of Wozniak and jealous of his new girlfriend Hyde. She may also have had access to Lauper's gun, but she is in Europe and not reachable.

The defense will call Chris Hyde, Savanah's brother, to testify about the rocky relationship between Savanah and Wozniak. He will also testify about Jan Butler's jealousy over Wozniak's relationship with Savanah.

Faulkner will testify in his own defense. He was there at the apartment complex that night because he was worried about Wozniak hurting Savanah, but he claims he had nothing to do with the murder. By the time he went into the apartment, he says, they were already dead.

It was an interesting case. Relatively simple, yet deeply nuanced, and challenging to both sides. Two principal witnesses for each side—Royce and Lauper for the prosecution, and Chris Hyde and Faulkner for the defense. Each witness with baggage, and fuel for the other side. A good case for a trial.

One small thing: It isn't real.

REFLECTIONS

In 2013, the international nongovernmental organization (NGO), Regional Dialogue, asked if I would travel to Uzbekistan on a pro bono basis, and work with lawyers and judges there on reforming their judicial system. Uzbekistan is a fascinating country. To the south, along the ancient "Silk Road" from China, are the beautiful mosques, buildings, and artistry of Samarkand and Bukhara. With a population of about 34 million, it is landlocked—surrounded by the other "stans": Afghanistan, Kazakhstan, Turkmenistan, etc. All the other "stans" have had serious troubles: social, political, economic and more. Uzbekistan has somehow flown under the radar and escaped the worst of it.

To be sure, in 2013, it was not a democracy. It had emerged from the Soviet empire with a president, Islam Karimov, who remained in office for twenty-five years and ruled with a strong hand. But it is also a country with a fairly young population, and many of its younger students and professionals longed for change. They knew they had to be extraordinarily patient and courageous. They listened carefully to every word of their president's speeches, searching for clues into how far they could push. Knowing that if they pushed too hard or too fast, it might create a backlash or worse. In 2016, Turkey, which had been engaged in a similar rule of law reform effort, cracked down viciously. In just one day, on July 16, 2016, some 2,745 judges were dismissed or detained, and it went on from there.

Among those wanting reform were lawyers. Uzbekistan had essentially the old Byzantine Inquisitorial system, where judges did almost everything. On the criminal side, the prosecution puts together a file, hands it to a judge, and the judge decides what to do with it from there. It was not entirely irrational: After all, the thinking goes, there is only one truth. The judge doesn't need two sets of lawyers getting in the way of the search for truth. So there were no real two-sided trials, no cross-examination, and few of the protections that we in the United States take for granted in our adversarial system. We try cases, or watch trials on TV or movies, and assume that's the way it works for everyone. It's not.

The younger lawyers in Uzbekistan were curious and wanted more. Without exposure to actual trials, much of what they thought they knew came from the few US movies and TV shows that made it through. But that's no way to explore real reform. So, the Regional Dialogue and its indominable leader, Mjusa Sever, were able to get permission to bring three of us from the United States in 2013 to help explain and demonstrate the adversarial system. For this purpose, I was able to persuade my friend, Harvard Law School professor Ron Sullivan, who ran Harvard's winter Trial Advocacy Workshop, where I had taught for many years, to allow me to bring the program to Uzbekistan and use one of their mock trial case files. That case was *State v. Faulkner*.

I took the long trip to Tashkent, the capital. But the main event of the trip was not there. It was at Lake Charvak, a resort area about a two-hour drive from Tashkent (it's a shorter drive now, since the roads have been improved, and you are less likely to have to stop, for example, as we did for a shepherd moving his flock of sheep down the road).

We took a group of about sixty lawyers and judges there for a three-day trial advocacy workshop and mock trial.

My first question was: Why? Time and money were precious for these programs. Why use so much of both to take them out of Tashkent: surely there are adequate hotels and conference spaces in the capital? The answer was surprising and enlightening: The further we can get them away from the capital, physically and psychologically, the freer they will feel to ask questions, explore new things, and speak their minds. That willingness to explore is what we were looking for.

So, we loaded everyone on buses and went to Charvak. Prosecutors, defense lawyers, private counsel, and judges. That in itself was a breakthrough: The four groups generally kept to themselves and rarely interacted. Slowly, they learned that they were all loyal Uzbekistanis, all lawyers, all interested in improving their system, and all trying to figure out how. The bus ride together, food, vodka, all that and more helped, but mostly it was just talking, listening, and spending time together.

We Americans had much to learn. We were not only there to teach about the adversarial system, but we also first had to **market** the adversarial system. I have lectured and taught cross-examination many times. But in Uzbekistan, before we could get to the "how" of cross, I had to present the "why." I had to sell this idea that it was more than some Hollywood trick: that it had an important purpose. The great US legal scholar, John Henry Wigmore, said, "Cross-examination is beyond any doubt the greatest legal engine ever invented for the discovery of truth."[1] But the Uzbekistanis were skeptical—they had to be convinced.

We spent about the first day and a half walking them through the key steps of a trial and other issues. We talked about the adversarial system, about the idea of a trial, in the words of its fifteenth-century origins, as the "Act or process of testing." Testing the truth from both sides. I used one of my favorite quotes, from the ancient fabulist Aesop, that, "Every truth has two sides; it is well to look at both, before we commit ourselves to either."[2] We then introduced them to opening, direct, cross, closing, and more. Then we spent the second half of day two introducing them to the Faulkner case, which had been translated for us into Uzbek. The basic facts. Two witnesses on each side. The process of a witness taking

---

[1] 3 Wigmore, Evidence §1367, p. 27 (2d ed. 1923).

[2] Aesop's Fables, *The Mule*, https://aesopsfables.org/F241_The-Mule.html.

the stand: direct, cross, redirect. How to plan and strategize the case. Then we broke them up into their trial teams to prepare (We actually had brought a second mock trial, as well, since we had so many people).

Imagine lawyers who know nothing about trials, attempting it for the first time. It was at times hilarious, confusing, profound, and enlightening. So much of what we—and they—learned from the experience reflected back on the lessons learned that we've discussed here. It's worth reflecting back on them, through the lens of the Uzbeks, and *State v. Faulkner.*

1. LAW AS A FORCE FOR CHANGE

- Farmers Export
- Appling County

The law is not static. If you believe in your case, you can often overcome substantial obstacles. You can push your side of the case as doing what's right. And even if you don't win, you have tried to do what's right. The other side will push back. Sometimes that can backfire, but often it is using our skills, and our system, to seek the right result.

We brought both the Farmers Export grain elevator explosion and the Appling County corruption prosecutions, knowing that we faced significant legal challenges. Knowing that we might lose, and losing such high-profile cases can not only set back the law, but it can also create martyrs out of the defendants. But we believed in both cases and pushed forward. In Appling County, we very nearly lost the case to the judge's concerns about the Racketeer Influenced and Corrupt Organizations (RICO) Act. In Farmers Export, the criminal regulatory statute was also controversial, and that controversy was proven by the hung jury. Both cases were right to bring, and both cases were "wins" in meaningful ways.

The Uzbeks had no sense of there being two sides to the story, or the notion that, in trial, either side might prevail. Prosecutors assembled and handed the judge the case file. If the file was inadequate for conviction, that reflected badly on the prosecutor—they might get disciplined or even fired. Our principles of burden of proof, presumption of innocence, and proof beyond a reasonable doubt were not commonly accepted.

On the afternoon of the second day of the workshop, while the trial teams met to plan out their trials, I walked around the large room with an interpreter, listening in and answering questions. Suddenly, one of the NGO staff came running from the other side of the room: "Mr. Small, we have a crisis! The prosecution team in the Faulkner case is quitting!" Puzzled, I replied: "What do you mean, quitting? It's just an exercise." "I don't know," he said, "please come with me!" So, I did.

The balance of power within the Uzbek judicial system at that time was still almost entirely with the prosecution. Prosecutors were government officials, and, until recently, had even worn military-type uniforms. I had not fully appreciated it in the larger group, but when I walked over to the table of six to eight prosecutors together, I realized that, effectively, they were still in uniform: all of them wore black suits, white shirts, and narrow ties. Combined with the clear sense of unhappiness around the table, it looked to me like a caricature of an undertakers convention. Grim.

Through the interpreter, I asked what the problem was. The lead prosecutors responded, "We cannot try this case, we might lose." In an essentially one-sided system, "losing" was not a tolerable option. To "lose" a case they put together and handed to the judge, would be an unheard of personal and professional rebuke. It just wasn't done, and they were not willing to start here.

I explained to them—as we had said all day—that this was just an exercise. No one was being evaluated or graded. That, like any mock trial case file, it was designed to be fair, to give both sides a chance to put on witnesses, to cross-examine witnesses, and to do so, having a chance to win in the end. In real life, they might decide not to even bring the case if it was too close. But here, they could relax: that decision had been made by others. And because it was so close, whoever took it most seriously, worked hardest, and planned hardest had a better chance at winning.

Still facing a skeptical audience, I launched into my best Vince Lombardi imitation, the great NFL football coach who famously said, "Winners never quit, and quitters never win."[3] Just because it's hard, I said, doesn't mean that you shouldn't try, just that you should try harder. I know this is a new world for you. We're here to help you try out something new, with no one telling you what to do or passing judgment on you, or carrying it over to your other work. Just offering to show you some options, some alternatives. Slowly, they overcame their doubts and fears, and ended up being enthusiastic participants.

---

[3] Vince Lombardi Quotes, BRAINYMEDIA INC (Nov. 6, 2023, https://www.brainy quote.com/quotes/vince_lombardi_122285.

Winning and losing. Pushing for what you believe is right, even though it may not be easy, or a sure thing. These are aspects of our system that we take for granted, but we should not. They allow us to do what's right, what we believe in, even when it's new, or unpopular, or challenging. To the Uzbeks, that was opening the door to a brand-new world. Scary but exciting.

2. CORE THEMES/STORYTELLING

- Gilbert
- SG Limited

In every case, we should talk to nonlawyers—friends, family, strangers—to develop the core themes and the story. The core themes are three to five short, clear, powerful statements that demonstrate to Juror #6 why we're here. In the Gilbert naval architect negligence case, that process helped us to understand the basic questions of the case and how to present them.

It's also important to have a story to tell and to fit the law and facts into that story. In SG Limited, the fun story of an internet game helped us to get the case dismissed by the US District Court, and then to overcome the negative legal ruling on appeal and push a very favorable result. Whenever possible, have a story to tell, and tell it well.

On the defense, particularly in a criminal matter, there are some cases where the defense is safest to rely on the burden of proof, and not present a story that can then be contradicted by the evidence. In one case I prosecuted as an Assistant US Attorney, I got frustrated at one point and complained to the judge that the defense story was incomplete and made no sense. Wise Judge Tauro leaned over the bench with a smile and said, "Mr. Small, I think that the theory of defense here is, 'prove it!'" A valid legal defense, but not the first choice, if there's an alternative story available.

In the Faulkner case, good counsel could develop good stories on both sides. The prosecution painted the picture of a jealous and jilted Faulkner, sitting in the lonely guard shack, staring up at Wozniak's apartment, while Wozniak slept with the love of Faulkner's life, until he could take it no longer. The defense, by contrast, could describe two hard-living, hard-drinking, sometime lovers, Wozniak and Hyde, getting into a wild argument in the middle of the night, which led to a murder-suicide.

With each team, prosecution and defense, we spent time talking through the story. Seeing where the pieces fit. At first, they came up with wild theories, but then we pushed them to look more carefully at the evidence, and mesh the evidence and the story. Eventually, they became excited by the process, working to paint the picture with the facts and watch out for the pitfalls.

Trials are about connections. Making the connections between witnesses, between facts, between pieces of the story. The great challenge of preparing for trial, the Uzbeks learned, is finding, exploring, and developing those connections. As an observer, it was a powerful reminder of the frustrations, challenges, and excitement of that process.

3. JUROR #6

- Cammarata

In the United States, we are used to seeing and hearing about juries. The challenge for trial lawyers is to break it down from a blob to real people: Juror #6. Who is he or she, why are they there, and what do they need from us? In Uzbekistan, trying the Faulkner case to a jury was going to be a completely new and foreign experience. Juries had simply not been part of their system of justice. But that was part of the menu of options of which we wanted to give them a taste.

We talked about the jury system: how they were selected, what their role was, how the process worked. Then, since we had more judges than we needed for the trial, we turned a group of judges into the jury. As discussed previously, judges play a major fact-finding role there, so they were the best candidates, as well. So, there they sat, twelve judges, transformed into jurors, performing a function previously unheard of in their system.

Of course, it was all new to the lawyers, as well. Spending most of a trial communicating with a jury mainly through questions to others, and their answers, is without a doubt a bizarre way to communicate. We in the United States are more accustomed to it, and to the thinking and planning that it requires. It's not a natural or easy way to tell a story, but it's the rules we live by: "Question, Pause, Answer, Stop."

That seemed too slow and too artificial for the Uzbeks. At first, some of the lawyers would ask a question of the witness, get an answer, then turn to the jury and explain the significance: "You see, this shows that the defendant was really . . ." Pretty soon, the other side would object, backing their objection up with their explanation, and we were off to the races. Sometimes it took a while to get order, and it took even longer to get them to understand that, strange as it might be, that was not the trial process.

Think about how tightly orchestrated a trial is, for the most part. It's nowhere near the freewheeling way that we carry on our normal lives, conversations, debates, whatever. In a conversation, the person asking you a question is the audience: they're the one you are speaking to and hoping to be understood by. In a trial, the questioner is not the real audience: the jurors are. It's an awkward, artificial process.

Frankly, we had put the judges on the jury mostly because we wanted a jury for the lawyers to speak to and didn't know what else to do with all those judges. We didn't fully consider the impact it would have on them. They were fascinated by the experience. Sometimes confused, sometimes frustrated, but focused and listening in ways they never would have as mere spectators. They desperately wanted to ask questions and were surprised when we explained that was usually not the process for juries. They were intrigued by the idea of "deliberating," and did so diligently. And then surprised everyone. In a system where a defendant, once charged, is rarely found innocent, they listened carefully to our instructions on the burden of proof and the jury's role and came back with a "verdict" of not guilty! I think even they were surprised.

4. FINDING COMMON GROUND WITH THE JUDGE

- Farmers Export
- Rendle

Judges in the United States wear many hats: decision-maker on substantive, procedural, and evidentiary law and facts, and much more. Once a case goes to trial, the judge also plays the important role of referee between the two sides: keeping order and enforcing the rules and—hopefully—fairness. So, it's important for a trial lawyer to find common ground with a judge based on respect and the rule of law.

In the Farmers Export case, that process started early in the trial: trying to respect a judge's strict courtroom etiquette while still enthusiastically advocating our case. In the Rendle case, it was an ongoing effort to strike a balance of mutual respect with a sometimes-difficult judge who I disagreed with often. In both cases, the general parameters of our respective roles were clear. It was a matter of exploring and respecting the friction points.

But since the Uzbek system did not have adversarial trials, judges had little or no experience in the role of referee between two sides. We selected one of the attending judges to preside over the Faulkner trial. But it was very quickly clear that she was lost in that role. We had been talking with the lawyers for two days about the adversarial system, about there being two sides, and about being a zealous advocate for your side. Some of the lawyers were not able to make the change, but some did and were enthusiastic advocates. It started getting out of control, and the judge had no experience with what to do.

I quickly realized that in our preparation for the workshop, we had not spent any time on the judge's referee role, and we had forgotten one key piece of that role: a gavel. So I grabbed a maintenance man and urgently requested a hammer. Fortunately, he had one handy, and I brought it up to the judge's "bench," showed her how to bang it as a gavel, and explained the gavel's all-important role in gaining attention—and respect—for the judge as referee. It took some further encouragement, but she eventually caught on and helped control the process much more effectively.

Imagine a hard-fought trial without a judge. Pretty nearly impossible. We in the United States may complain that some judges are too strict, some judges are too lenient. But we understand the importance of that "referee" role to our system of justice. Like a baseball game without an umpire: someone has to call balls and strikes, or the game cannot go forward. Without trials, the Uzbeks had little need for referees. Yet another key part of the process they needed to develop to make all the pieces fit.

5. BRING OUT THE BAD STUFF (BOBS)

- Appling County

Few witnesses are perfect—in what they've said or done in the case, or in the past. Many have things in their past that they are embarrassed—or worse—to talk about in open court. Yet those things may be discoverable by the other side and helpful to their cross-examination. Without diving into the various rules here, prior convictions, prior bad acts, prior inconsistent statements, and more can be important points in assessing credibility on cross-examination.

In that environment, the worst thing a witness can do is try to hide anything. It's the old Watergate scandal maxim, that the coverup can be worse than the crime. At the very least, it can take a manageable issue, and make it far worse, by allowing the other side to be the one to bring it up, with a flourish and with an attack that the witness tried to keep it from the jury. For that reason, it's so important for the witness to tell counsel everything—good or bad—and for counsel to be sure to bring it out, in the best possible light.

BOBS was the acronym we used when I was a prosecutor: "Bring Out the Bad Stuff." In the Appling County case, Billy Breen was the ultimate candidate for BOBS—a high-level career criminal who had only recently changed sides. The first challenge was getting him to accept his history and then working with him to testify about it to the jury. In the end, his shocking but complete honesty saved him as a witness.

In Faulkner, both sides have a BOBS problem. Both the government's key witness Shaun Royce, and the defendant himself, have prior criminal convictions. Interestingly, both the prosecution and defense teams were initially vehement about not wanting to bring this up with their own witnesses. We can't be the ones to destroy our own witness's credibility, they argued. And a prior criminal conviction would surely do just that.

Throughout this exercise, we worked hard to not tell the Uzbek lawyers what to do, not tell them what was the "right way" or the "wrong way." If they were going to explore this new adversarial process, it was important that they try to work these issues out themselves. Our job was to provide information, suggestions, and guidance to help them along. Those discussions were sometimes the most interesting and the most productive.

We suggested that since the fact of the convictions was known to the other side, keeping it a secret was not an option. They probably did not have the choice to keep it out entirely—that choice was up to the court, which had ruled against them. The choice they might have is to control how and when the convictions came out and that timing was essential to both their, and their witness's, credibility. Eventually, they understood, and offered their witness's flaws, with explanation, on direct examination. And in so doing, they learned that it took much of the sting out of the issue for cross-examination.

6. CROSS-EXAMINATION

- Farmers Export
- Appling County

The Confrontation Clause of the Sixth Amendment to the US Constitution requires that in all criminal prosecutions, the accused shall enjoy the right to be confronted by the witnesses against him. But the idea of examining witnesses to find the truth goes back much further.

A wonderful early example is in the Bible's Book of Daniel, chapter 13, recounting the story of Susanna and the elders. Two old men who had attempted, unsuccessfully, to seduce Susanna, a beautiful married woman, thereafter bore witness to the people of their tribe that she had accepted the attentions of a young man. The people were about to put her to death when young Daniel intervened, saying, "Are ye so foolish, ye children of Israel, that without examination or knowledge of the truth, you have condemned a daughter of Israel?"[4] He then questioned the two elders out of each others' presence (a precursor to today's courts' sequestration rules!) about where the alleged event had taken place, and when they gave conflicting answers, Susanna was absolved and the old men condemned.

Cross-examination is at the heart of our adversarial system. Not just in criminal cases: many civil cases are decided at least in part based on cross-examination of a key witness. Indeed, many depositions, as a chance to challenge an opposing witness, are themselves largely a form of cross-examination. In the Farmers Export case, the cross of the defense expert, and the defense 'bridge' witness, were major turning points. In the Appling County case, cross delivered the "good lickin'" the jury felt defendant AZ Jackson deserved.

But in Uzbekistan, there was little experience with, or understanding of, cross-examination in a trial setting. And pretty much any questioning of witnesses was a one-way street: the government as part of its investigation.

---

[4] *Daniel* 13:48.

So, when we explained that the mock trial was a criminal case, in which both sides would call two witnesses, and both sides would cross-examine the other side's two witnesses, that was very new and surprising. We had already talked about cross-examination, and we went through the case file extensively, to make sure that everyone understood what would happen. Then we split them up into their trial teams so they could prepare for trial, including who on each team would be doing which parts of the trial.

But it's hard to overcome a lifetime of experience in two days. I can promise you the moon, but will you really believe me? Defense counsel at that time there had little power to do anything more than hold their client's hand as they went off to jail. Putting on witnesses? Questioning witnesses? Promise me the moon.

That night of the second day of the workshop, the night before trial, I was sitting at dinner with my interpreter and a table of defense lawyers. At one point in the conversation, one of the brightest and most sophisticated lawyers in the group, turned to me and said through an interpreter, "Mr. Small, we are not really going to ask questions of a government witness tomorrow, right?" I was surprised by her question since that was what we had been talking about for two days. I replied, "Yes, as we've discussed, both sides will call two witnesses, and you should be prepared to cross-examine the government's two witnesses. That's what will happen."

And after a difficult pause, this mature, intelligent lawyer, started to cry. "I'm sorry for my tears, Mr. Small," she said, "But do you think that could ever happen in my country: that a defense lawyer could actually ask questions of a government witness?" I had to be honest with her. "I don't know," I said. "I know that seems like a long way away, and I'm not here from the United States to tell another country what they should or should not do. But I know there is interest in this, I believe in it, and we are here to show you what some of the options are, to show you what's possible, in the hope that you will consider the choices, and choose what is best for Uzbekistan." And she wiped away her tears and said, "Thank you so much for coming here to help us!" The next day in trial, she did a damn good job in her first cross-examination of a government witness.

We take so much for granted . . . Shame on us. Lessons learned.

Epilogue

Ten years after this first workshop, in April 2023, after several more trips to Uzbekistan, hosting and speaking to several delegations in the United States, and various remote presentations, I was honored to be asked to speak at an International Conference in Tashkent, in anticipation of a national referendum on amendments to the Uzbek Constitution. I had been asked to review and comment on the amendments the summer before, and since then they had passed both houses of Parliament and a review by the Constitutional Court. Now, representatives from seventeen countries were gathered to speak in favor of the amendments, and talk about reform and the Rule of Law. It was an extraordinary and moving event, knowing how far they had come, and how hard people had worked to get them there.

The Amendments are sweeping changes in many aspects of life. In the judicial system, ten years after counsel had to wipe away tears at her inability to effectively represent her clients, they include:

- The presumption of innocence
- The privilege against self-incrimination
- The right to effective counsel
- The right to trial
- And yes, amazingly enough, the right of a criminal defendant to confront and question witnesses against them.

It has been an extraordinary process to witness—and assist in some small way. Some of the pieces of our system that seemed so alien and impossible to them at first have now become accepted or desired. Some of those patient and courageous young reformers are now senior officials in the government and the courts. The NGO Regional Dialogue's pioneering efforts have become so widely respected and requested that they now have a large staff on the ground in Uzbekistan and formed an Advisory Council to help them plan and develop future programs, which they asked me to join.

Uzbekistan still has a long way to go, to turn these high goals into day-to-day reality across the country. What country does not have its struggles? I've had the privilege of watching them come so far, and whatever the many lawyers and judges I've worked with there have learned from me, I have also learned from them. With each interaction, I am reminded that what they are hoping for, striving for, we as trial lawyers too often take for granted. Every trial lawyer has a responsibility to treat the system with respect and do what they can to make it better. The Uzbeks look to us as a role model, for better and for worse, for many of the things they want to consider for their system, and for how some of those good things can be too easily abused. We need to be more aware of that fragile balance on a daily basis.

Lessons learned.